MASTERS OF MUSIC
CHOPIN
AND ROMANTIC MUSIC

TEXT BY:
CARLO CAVALLETTI

ILLUSTRATIONS BY:
STUDIO INKLINK, MATTEO CHESI,
CESARE D'ANTONIO, GIACOMO SORIANI

BARRON'S

DoGi

English translation
© Copyright 2000
by Barron's Educational
Series, Inc.
Original edition © 1999 by
DoGi spa, Florence, Italy
Title of original edition:
*Chopin e la musica
romantica*
Italian edition by:
Carlo Cavalletti
Editor:
Francesco Milo
Graphic display:
Romano Rizzato
Illustrations:
Studio Inklink,
Matteo Chesi,
Giacomo Soriani,
Cesare D'Antonio
Art director and page
makeup:
Sebastiano Ranchetti
Iconographic researcher:
Katherine Carson Forden

Translation from Italian by:
Anna Maria Salmeri
Pherson

HOW TO READ THIS BOOK

Every facing page is a chapter on Chopin's musical art and life, other great musicians of the romantic era, and/or the great events of the musical culture of their times. The text above on the left (1) and the large illustration in the middle, deal with the main subject. The text in italics (2) recounts in chronological order the life of Chopin. The other elements on the page—photos, reproductions of prints of the times, and portraits—complement the information.*

ACKNOWLEDGMENTS

ABBREVIATIONS:
t: (top) / **b**: (below) / **c**: (center) / **r**: (right) /
l: (left)

ILLUSTRATIONS:
The illustrations in this volume are new and
original. They were developed by DoGi spa,
which owns its copyright.
ART BY: Studio Inklink (Simone Boni,
Alessandro Rabatti, Lorenzo Pieri, Luigi
Critone, Francesco Petracchi, Lucia Mattioli,
Theo Caneschi, Federico Ferniani) : 4–5,
6–7, 10–11, 12–13, 16–17, 18–19, 22–23,
30–31, 34–35, 40–41, 42–43, 47tl, 48–49,
50–51, 52–53, 53tr, 56–57, 58–59, 60–61;
Cesare D'Antonio: 8–9, 32–33, 44–45, 54–55;
Matteo Chesi: 14–15, 20–21, 24–25, 28–29,
36–37; Giacomo Soriani: 26–27, 46–47; Walter
Angelici: 38–39; Alessandro Menchi, 12tl.

COVER: Studio Inklink
FRONTISPIECE: Studio Inklink

LIST OF REPRODUCTIONS:
DoGi spa has done its best to discover possible rights of third parties. We apologize for
any omissions or mistakes, and we will be
pleased to introduce the appropriate correc-
tions in the later editions of this book.
(The works reproduced in their totality are
followed by the consonant a (all); those par-
tially reproduced are followed by the consonant d (detail).

6t *G.W.F. Hegel*, engraving (ARCHIVIO DOGI)
d; **6b** Print from a painting by Joseph Carl
Stieler, *Friedrich Schelling*, a lithography
(HISTORISCHES MUSEUM DER STADT, VIENNA) a;
7 Joseph Carl Stieler, *J. L. Tieck* (ARCHIVIO
DOGI) d; **8b** Joseph Carl Stieler,
Johann Wolfgang Goethe, oil painting (NEUE
PINAKOTHEK, MUNICH) d; **10** M. Fajans, *Joseph
Elsner*, engraving (SOCIÉTÉ HISTORIQUE ET
LITTÉRAIRE POLONAISE, PARIS) d; **11** J. Lewicki,
The Celebration of the Harvest in Poland, oil
painting (SOCIÉTÉ HISTORIQUE ET LITTÉRAIRE
POLONAISE, PARIS) d; **14t** Caroline Bardua,
Carl Maria von Weber, oil (AKG, BERLIN) d;
14b *E. T. A. Hoffmann*, drawing (IGDA,
MILAN) a; **15** *Richard Wagner*, 1868 (HULTON
DEUTSCH COLLECTION) a; **16** *Bedrich Smetana*
(MUSEUM SMETANA, PRAGUE) d; **17l** Anony-
mous, *Masonry Symbols on a Master's Apron*,
XVIII c., silk (AKG/BERLIN); **17r** *Karl Marx*
(ARCHIVIO DOGI) d; **19l** *Musical Evening*
(ARCHIVIO DOGI) a; **19r** *Charles Gounod*
(ARCHIVIO DOGI) a; **20** Anonymous, *Robert
Schumann and Clara Wieck*, engraving from
daguerreotype, 1847 (HULTON DEUTSCH/
BELTMANN) a; **21** Gabor Melegh, *Franz
Schubert*, oil (ARCHIVIO DOGI) a; **22** Anony-
mous, *William Shakespeare*, oil (ARCHIVIO
DOGI) d; **23** A. L. Girodet-Trioson,
Chateaubriand, oil (MUSÉE DE VERSAILLES) a;
24 Mantour, *Caricature of Paganini* (PRIVATE
COLLECTION) a; **25** Pierre de Pommayrac,
Paganini, miniature (PALACE DORIA-TURSI,
GENOA) d; **26** Gioachino Rossini (ARCHIVIO
DOGI) a; **27l** C. Moyaux, *Audition in the
Room of the Paris Conservatory*, watercolor
(COLLECTION ANDRÉ MEYWE, PARIS) d; **27r**
Vincenzo Bellini, (BIBLIOTHÈQUE NATIONALE,

PARIS) a; **28** Marie-Alexandre Alophe, *Marie
Moke*, a lithography (IGDA, MILAN) a; **29**
Anonymous, Hector Berlioz in a caricature
from the journal of the Vienna Theater
(OSTERREICHISCHEN NATIONAL BIBLIOTHEK,
VIENNA) a; **30** Anonymous, *Giacomo
Meyerbeer*, a lithography (IGDA, MILAN) a; **31**
Anonymous, *Eugène Scribe*, a lithography
(BIBLIOTHÈQUE NATIONAL, PARIS) a; **32**
Eugène Delacroix, *Faust with Marguerite in
Prison*, a lithography (BIBLIOTHÈQUE NATIONAL,
PARIS) d; **33** Gabor Melegh, *Franz Schubert*,
oil (GALERIE NATIONALE DES BEWUX-ARTS DE
HONGRIE) d; **34** Anonymous, *Clara Wieck
Schumann*, oil (IGDA, MILA) d; **36** Anony-
mous, *Robert Schumann*, oil (ROBERT
SCHUMANN HAUS, ZWICKAU) d; **37**
Johannes Brahms, daguerreotype (DEUTSCHE
STAATBIBLIOTHEK, BERLIN), d; **39** *Harpsichord
of J. A. Stein* (ACCADEMIA BARTOLOMEO
CRISTOFORI, FLORENCE) a; **40l** Carl Hatmann,
Franz Liszt, watercolor (LISZT' HOUSE,
WEIMAR) d; **40r** Anonymous, *Caricature of
Liszt* (STADTARCHIV, WEIMAR) a; **41** Anony-
mous, *Liszt* (COLLECTION ERNST BURGER,
MUNICH) d; **42** Robert Koch (ARCHIVIO
DOGI) a; **43** Eugène Delacroix, *Frédéric
Chopin*, oil (LOUVRE, PARIS) d; **44** Mayer,
John Field, engraving (HULTON DEUTSCH
COLLECTION) a; **45** L. Eisherzy, *Novalis*,
engraving (IGDA, MILAN) a; **46** Anonymous,
Weber Conducts the Free Shooter, engraving
(DAGLI ORTI, MILAN) d; **47r** Hans von Bülow
(IGDA, MILAN) a; **48t** Page of the score of
Liszt's Sonata (ARCHIVIO DOGI) a; **48b**
Kazimierz Zaleski, *The Market Square of Old
Warsaw* (HISTORICAL MUSEUM, WARSAW) d;

49 T. Kwiatkowski, *Chopin in a Dressing
Gown at the Piano*, watercolor (NATIONAL
LIBRARY OF WARSAW) d; **50** Anonymous, *View
of Leipzig*, watercolored engraving (BACH-
ARCHIV, LEIPZIG) d; **51** Anonymous, *Edvard
Grieg*, oil (AKG, BERLIN) d; **53** Anonymous,
Carl Czerny, engraving (IGDA, MILAN) a; **54**
Ludwig Spohr, *Pastel Self-Portrait* (LANDES-
MUSEUM, BRAUNSCHWEIG) d; **55l** W.J. Mahler,
Ludwig von Beethoven, oil (HISTORISCHES
MUSEUM DER STADT, VIENNA) d; **55r** Anony-
mous, *Johannes Brahms*, oil (AKG, BERLIN) d;
57 Frontispiece of the *Polonaise-Fantaisie*,
op. 61 (BRITISH LIBRARY, LONDON) a; **58t** Page
of the autographed score of the *Fourth
Symphony in D Minor*, op. 120 by Schumann
(BILDARCHIV PREUSSISCHER KULTURBESITZ,
BERLIN) a; **58b** Robert Burns, *Lord George
Byron*, oil (MARY EVANS PICTURE LIBRARY,
LONDON) d; **59** Ferdinand Schmutzer,
Richard Strauss, engraving (PROF. RUDOLF
HARTMANN, MUNICH) a; **60** *Frédéric Chopin*,
daguerreotype (BIBLIOTHÈQUE POLONAISE,
PARIS) d; **61** Leonid Pasternak, *Sergej
Rachmaninov*, drawing (GALLERY TRETJAKOV,
MOSCAU) d.

COVER (from left to right):
1. 8b; **2.** 32; **3.** 14b; **4.** 49; **5.** 29; **6.** 34; **7.**
45; **8.** 55r; **9.** 19l; **10.** 11; **11.** 21; **12.** 27l;
13. 17l; **14.** 58b; **15.** 33; **16.** 24

BACK COVER:
Eugène Delacroix, *Frédéric Chopin*, 1838,
oil (LOUVRE, PARIS) a.

CONTENTS

THE PROTAGONISTS

At the end of the 1820s, slightly behind the movement in literature, romantic music became a major force in Germany. It soon echoed all over Europe, accompanying nationalistic outbreaks that would shake the century. Romanticism became rooted more deeply in instrumental music in German-language areas, while French and Italian music centered primarily around opera. Romantic individualism was expressed by the sound of the piano. Both virtuosos, who amazed their audiences with their technical skills, and poets, who trusted their most subdued emotions to its sound, preferred the piano. Paris, which was home to the latest state-of-the-art piano makers and the most extraordinary performers of the time, among whom included Chopin, became the capital of the piano.

✦ **HECTOR BERLIOZ** (1803–1869) The only Frenchman among the great romantics, he largely influenced orchestral writing.

✦ **NICCOLÒ PAGANINI** (1782–1840) **AND FRANZ LISZT** (1811–1886) Their transcendental virtuosity swept across Europe and created the legend of the great solo performer.

✦ **CARL MARIA VON WEBER** (1786–1826) **AND GIACOMO MEYERBEER** (1791–1864) Weber created German romantic opera and Meyerbeer French grand opera.

✦ **FELIX MENDELSSOHN** (1809–1847) A complete, refined, and elegant musician, Mendelssohn embodied the most balanced side of romanticism.

✦ **ROBERT SCHUMANN** (1810–1856) Schumann was a multifaceted genius, tormented by madness, who resembled the fictional character of a romantic novel.

✦ **GEORGE SAND** (1804–1876) **AND CLARA WIECK** (1819–1896) Sand was a successful writer and Chopin's lover; Wieck was a gifted pianist, with whom Schumann was in love.

✦ **PRECURSORS OF GERMAN ROMANTICISM**
Hegel (1770–1831), Novalis (1772–1801), Tieck (1773–1853), Hoffmann (1776–1822), August-Wilhelm Schlegel (1767–1845), and his brother Friedrich (1772–1829) were some of the literary figures who developed a new conception of the poet and artist, and the supremacy of music over the other arts.

✦ **FRÉDÉRIC CHOPIN**
Born in Poland in 1810, Chopin went to live in Paris in 1831. He died there of tuberculosis in 1849. He wrote only piano compositions.

✦ **EUGÈNE DELACROIX** (1798–1863) **AND VICTOR HUGO** (1802–1885)
A few years older than Chopin, they are considered the fathers of French romanticism in the fields of painting and literature. Delacroix was Chopin's only friend in Paris.

✦ **SÉBASTIEN ERARD** (1752–1831) **AND IGNAZ PLEYEL** (1757–1831)
Founders of the two most important Parisian piano companies, they offered new stimuli to composers because of their technical innovations. They contributed to the evolution of the language of the piano.

GERMAN ROMANTIC THEORY

In the nineteenth century, the poet and essayist Friedrich Schlegel gave new meaning to the term *romantic*, formerly used to describe landscapes or emotions. It came to describe a new form of poetry that was in conflict with the ancient or classical form. The different romantic trends seen in Germany shared the same conception of art as an outpouring of feelings. They valued creative freedom rather than rational expression or the classical idea of beauty, and favored symbols, history, and legend. Moved by their spiritualism, the romantics refused all codified forms. They scorned a society that was apparently incapable of recognizing the new values. Being pure and absolute, instrumental music rose to become a sublime art. It stands out as the original language of nature, capable of interpreting human feelings and telling what language cannot express.

♦ THE ROMANTIC YEARNING
Romanticism replaced rationality, once seen as the finished force that was able to gradually transform the world, with a spiritual, creative, and infinite principle. The philosophers Hegel (above) and Fichte attributed this principle to an absolute and superior reason, whose manifestations were the objects of philosophy. On the other hand, such literary figures as Tieck and Novalis yearned for the feeling that best reveals itself in art and religion. In contrast with the cosmopolitanism of the eighteenth century, the nineteenth century was the age of the rediscovery of traditions, legends, and the spiritual heritage of each nation. On the political level, this promoted an awareness of national identities, the first step toward the creation of contemporary states.

♦ CASPAR DAVID FRIEDRICH
(1774–1840) Friedrich was the most influential figure of romantic art in Germany. He believed that the spiritual ego was the only resource of men and artists.

♦ ATHENAEUM
This was a literary review published from 1798 to 1800 by the Schlegels in collaboration with Schelling (opposite) and Novalis. It voiced the early romanticism theory shared by the Jena circle, that poetry reflects time and its movement.

♦ THE WANDERER ABOVE THE SEA OF FOG AND THE MONK BY THE SEA
These two famous paintings reflect the solitude that men feel when facing an immense, primordial, and unspoiled nature.

IN THE PAINTER'S STUDIO
Dresden, 1818. Visiting the painter Friedrich, as reserved and lonely as his paintings and studio, the poet and musician, Hoffmann, admired the barren landscapes.

♦ ROMANTIC LITERATURE
The origin of romantic literature is *Sturm und Drang*, the literary movement named after Klinger's drama of 1776, which influenced even the young Goethe and Schiller. The reevaluation of passion, the call for more freedom in poetry, and the revival of true German cultural sources instead of the enlightened and classical French models, were already present. Among the greatest romantic literary figures are Novalis (1772–1801), author of *Hymn to Night*, in which he blended the themes of death, love, and mysticism, and J. L. Tieck (1773–1853) (above, in a portrait), mostly known for his medieval stories and fantasies. The Parisian Mme. De Stäel (1776–1817) introduced with her *From Germany* (1810) German theories of romanticism in France and Italy.

♦ FAIRY TALES
Published in 1812, these tales were patiently collected by Jacob (1785–1863) and Wilhelm (1786–1859) Grimm, the spiritual leaders of the romantic circle of Heidelberg. This group investigated the origins and early forms of German culture.

♦ E. T. A. HOFFMANN
(1776–1822) Hoffmann was a poet, writer, composer, and orchestra director. He wrote the *Fantastic Tales* and discovered the expressive characteristics of romantic music in Mozart and Beethoven.

CHOPIN'S LIFE

1. ♦ *Frédéric Francois Chopin was born on February 22, 1810, at Zelazowa-Wola, Poland, about 31 miles (50 km) from Warsaw. Encouraged to play the piano first by his mother and then by his sister Ludwika, who was four years older than he, he continued his training in 1816, under Wojciech Zywny. In 1817 he composed his first known composition, the* Polonaise in G Minor. *On February 24, 1818, he debuted with the* Concerto in E Minor *by Adalbert Gyrowetz at a charitable event in the theater of the Radziwill Palace.* ➤➤

THE MENDELSSOHNS

♦ **MENDELSSOHN**
Born in 1809 in Hamburg, Felix Mendelssohn Bartholdy (the last name was added after the family's conversion to Christianity) had already composed, by age 15, symphonies, concertos, two operas, piano music, and chamber music. At 17, he composed a masterpiece, the overture to Shakespeare's *A Midsummer Night's Dream*. An excellent pianist and orchestra director, at age 20, he performed Bach's long-forgotten *St. Matthew Passion*. His performance led to rediscovery of Bach's music. After studying in England and, upon Goethe's advice, in Italy, he returned many times to England, always to enthusiastic crowds. After serving as director of the Düsseldorf Conservatory for two years, he went to Leipzig in 1835. There he became the conductor of the Gewandhaus Orchestra, founded the local Conservatory of Music, and died at the age of 38. Above, his portrait.

The Mendelssohns were a family of Jewish bankers who had become wealthy after the reestablishment of civil rights in Germany following the French Revolution. They subsequently converted to the Protestant faith. Felix Mendelssohn grew up in an environment that was highly representative of this new society and its cultivated and bourgeois aspirations. With his brothers, he studied painting, literature, and music. The most influential intellectuals of the time visited his family's home while he was still a child: The poet Heinrich Heine, writer and philosopher, Jacob Grimm, historian Gustav Droysen, literary critic and historian August-Wilhelm Schlegel, and Friedrich Schlegel, who had married his aunt, Dorothea Mendelssohn. Karl Friedrich Zelter, Goethe's friend and musical advisor, taught him composition.

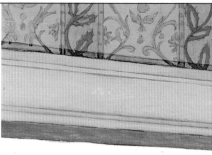

♦ **KARL FRIEDRICH ZELTER** (1758–1832) Zelter passed on his love for the music of Johann Sebastian Bach to his student, Mendelssohn.

LITERARY INTERLUDES AND TEA
Winter 1825, Berlin. In the dining room of the Mendelssohns, Hegel, Humboldt, and Tieck wrote literary pieces and brief poems for the homespun magazine founded by young Felix and his friends. In summer, its title was changed to "The Garden Journal."

♦ **JOHANN WOLFGANG VON GOETHE** (1749–1832). Goethe considered everything romantic as being "sick." The romantics, however, adored him, especially his novel, *The Sorrows of Young Werther* (1774) and his drama *Faust* (1808–1832). The 12-year-old Felix would play for him, becoming one of his friends.

♦ **HIS BELOVED FANNY** Mendelssohn's sister was an excellent pianist and a refined composer of chamber music and *Lieder* (songs).

♦ MOSES MENDELSSOHN
(1729–1786)
Felix's grandfather and an enlightened philosopher, he was called the "Jewish Socrates." He fought against the religious intolerance of eighteenth-century Prussia.

♦ WILHELM VON HUMBOLDT
(1767–1835)
Literary figure and liberal minister of education and religion, he founded the University of Berlin in 1810.

♦ GEORG WILHELM FRIEDRICH HEGEL
(1770–1831)
Hegel was one of the most influential intellectuals of German idealism. He considered music inner expression and a romantic art form. Felix attended his philosophy classes.

♦ JOHANN LUDWIG TIECK
(1773–1853)
A friend of the writers Wackenroder, Novalis, and the Schlegels, Tieck produced German editions of Shakespeare's works.

POLAND

At the beginning of the nineteenth century, the Grand Duchy of Warsaw was all that was left of the ancient Polish realm. The splendors of the sixteenth century were gone and the country was under the direct control of France. In 1815, Russia, the most backward of the allied nations, took over Poland in accordance with Vienna's deliberations. In November 1815, Czar Alexander I granted the constitution and the use of its language to the Polish people. They would be only formal acts; in fact, he appointed a Russian viceroy and a minister who had full power, destroyed the press, set up special courts of justice, and suspended the parliament that had protested against these measures for four years. In this climate, the romantic poets Adam Mickiewicz, Julius Slowacki, and Zygmunt Krasinski started to develop a Polish literature that dealt with mystical-historical themes. These were to be the seeds of a national identity.

♦ NICOLAS CHOPIN
Born near Nancy, France, in 1771, Chopin's father, Nicolas, moved to Poland in 1787. He taught French at the Warsaw Lycée and accepted board-ing students in his own home.

2. CHOPIN'S LIFE ♦ *In 1821 he composed the* Polonaise in A Flat Minor, *his first important work. In 1822 he studied composition with Joseph Elsner, and one year later he enrolled in the Warsaw Lycée. He often per-formed for the aristocracy. He spent his vacations in Kujawia, where he listened to folk music. In 1825 he published one of his compositions for the first time, the* Rondo in C Minor, *op. 1, and in 1826 after the Lycée, he formally enrolled in the Warsaw Music School and composed the* Polonaise in B Flat Minor. ≫→

♦ **EMILIA AND THE OTHER SISTERS**
Ludwika was born in 1807, Isabel in 1811, and Emilia in 1812. Emilia, gifted with an extraordinary literary talent, died at fourteen of tuberculosis.

♦ **CHOPIN'S BEST FRIENDS**
Titus Woyciechowski, Jan Matuszynski, and Julian Fontana, boarders of the Chopins and Frédéric's comrades, remained his lifelong friends.

♦ **FOLK MUSIC**
Beginning in the eighteenth century, folk tradition influenced Polish cultivated music. One of its typical traits is the irregularity of the rhythm, the so-called *rubato*, recognizable by its changes in speed against rhythmic accompaniments. The main dance rhythms of Polish music are the *Krakowiak*, in binary tempo, characterized by the syncopated rhythm of alternating movements of groups and solos; the *mazurek*, moderate and in triple meter, named after Mazowia, an area in Warsaw; the more common term of *mazurka* is of Russian origin. The more composed *polonaise*, the *oberek*, a vivacious dance, and the *kujiavak*, a more melancholy type of *mazurka* are also in triple meter. Above, a Polish folk scene.

THE EVOLUTION OF THE PIANO

From 1820 to 1850 the piano's look changed. Its technical features became more refined, the hammers and frame were made from different materials, the number and size of the pedals changed, the size, position, and tension of the strings varied, and the keyboard was made larger. These modifications led to an evolution in piano writing and technicality, as well as to new demands for piano concertos. Now, pianos were played in theaters and in very large concert halls, and accompanied full orchestras. This met the demands of the new rapidly expanding middle-class audience that relied on intellectuals and artists for producing and spreading ideas on a larger scale.

THE PLEYEL COMPANY IN PARIS
Located in the rue Cadet, not far from Montmartre, the company's studio was equipped in 1830 with a concert room, where the most important musicians of the day performed. In 1838 it was inaugurated as the *Salle* Pleyel, the new center of Parisian concert life.

♦ **FRENCH PIANOS**
In the 1830s Paris became the capital of the piano because it hosted the major virtuosos of the day as well as piano manufacturers such as Pleyel and Érard. The Pleyel company was founded in Paris in 1807 by Ignaz Pleyel (1757–1831), an Austrian musician and composer and a student of Haydn. Later, his son, Camille Pleyel, would manage it. Sébastien Érard (1752–1831) opened his Parisian factory in 1796. His greatest invention, patented in 1821, was the double-escapement action, which allows a note to be replayed before the key falls back to its original position, and which therefore allows performers to play very fast repetitions, trills, tremolos, and other embellishments. Above, the piano that Érard gave to Beethoven in 1804.

♦ **CAMILLE PLEYEL** (1788–1855). In 1839 Chopin dedicated the *24 Preludes*, op. 28 to Pleyel. The piano manufacturer would marry the young pianist Camille Moke, Berlioz's former fiancée.

♦ **PIANO PRODUCTION** During the nineteenth century, Pleyel and Érard each manufactured almost 100,000 pianos.

♦ **THE FRAME** The frame maintains the tension of the strings. It was during these years that metal bracing was introduced to support the strings.

♦ **THE STRINGS** Angle and length changed, caliber and tension increased, and the sound and volume grew.

♦THE KEYBOARD
Gradually, the
length of the
keyboard

increased. Felt-
tipped hammers
allowed for more
variation in sound.

♦THE PEDALS
The sustaining
or loud pedal
(the right pedal)
raises dampers
to sustain sound
and modify its
quality.

WEBER AND GERMAN ROMANTIC OPERA

In Germany, by the mid-eighteenth century, a new type of opera became popular—the *Singspiel*. These had a libretto written in German, with spoken roles instead of recitatives, folk topics, and simple musical structures influenced by popular melodies. Originally considered a "low" genre, the *Singspiel* rose to an artistic level thanks to Mozart and Beethoven. The first romantic masterpiece of this kind is *Der Freischütz* (*The Freeshooter*) by Carl Maria von Weber, brought to the Berlin theater on June 18, 1821, under the direction of the composer. Among those in the theater were Heine, Hoffmann, and the twelve-year-old Mendelssohn. In seven months the piece was performed fifty times. One year later, it was performed in thirty different theaters.

♦ **WEBER**
Born in Holstein in 1786, student of the Abbé Vogler and Michael Haydn, Weber was a renowned pianist and musical director. He was concertmaster in Breslau, Stuttgart, Prague, and Dresden. He changed the customs of these theaters, taking great care in the shows' musical preparation, their decor, lights, and singers' performances. He was also a critic and attempted to write a biographical novel, *The Life of a Musical Artist*, never finished. After *The Freeshooter*, Weber (above) completed *Euryanthe* for Vienna and *Oberon* for London, where he died of tuberculosis in 1826. He composed two concertos for piano and one *Konzertstück* for orchestra, four sonatas, and other works. The two concertos and the *Concertino for Clarinet* show the predominant role of the wind instruments and Weber's orchestral brilliance.

♦ **ERNST THEODOR AMADEUS HOFFMANN**
Poet, draftsman, musical critic, composer, and orchestra director, E. T. A. Hoffmann (1776–1822) was one of the precursors of German romantic opera with his work, *Ondine* (1816).

SAMIEL, THE DEMON
In the second act of *The Freeshooter*, Caspar, the lead character, calls out at midnight for Samiel, the demon to whom he has sold his soul. In order to live longer, he sacrifices his friend Max, to whom he has promised enchanted bullets.

♦ **THE NIGHT**
A typical romantic element of *The Freeshooter* is the frequent use of night scenes. "Half of the work takes place in darkness," Weber writes.

♦ **GOTHIC THEMES**
Other typical elements of German romantic opera are demons, witches, spells, and sorcery, which led up to *The Vampire*, written in 1828 by Heinrich Marschner.

♦ **AFTER WEBER: RICHARD WAGNER**
Chopin wrote no operas; Mendelssohn and Liszt wrote them only during their adolescent years. Schumann is the only one of the four great romantics to write for the theater, which he did later in life with *Genoveva*, inspired by one of Tieck's dramas and staged with small success in 1850. In those years, Richard Wagner (1813–1883) finished three works, called romantic for their fantastic and legendary themes in Weber's style. They are: *The Flying Dutchman*, *Tannhäuser*, and *Lohengrin*, performed for the first time in 1850, with Liszt as the conductor. Later, Wagner (above) radically changed opera's musical and theatrical levels with *Tristan and Isolde*, and the tetralogy, *Der Ring des Nibelungen* (*The Ring of the Nibelung*) (1876). In so doing, he influenced the entire European culture from the nineteenth to the beginning of the twentieth century.

THE ORCHESTRA
To emphasize demonic powers, Weber used the deepest notes of violins, violas, double basses, clarinets, bassoons, and horns, and gloomy timpanic sounds.

Europe 1820–1850: National Uprisings

The Restoration was the attempt of Austria, England, Prussia, and Russia to reestablish the order that had existed before the French Revolution and the Napoleonic wars. It proved to be unable to repress the new middle classes and the fevers of nationalism breaking out everywhere and manifested in romantic art. All over Europe, movements grew, popularizing the principle of sovereignty of the people. In France, Belgium, and Switzerland, where the social structure was more modern and the capitalistic development more advanced, they succeeded; elsewhere, as in Poland, they failed. In January 1831, national independence was proclaimed after an insurrection led by the military who were part of secret societies. Russia reacted by suppressing administrative autonomy and political freedom.

♦ MUSICAL NATIONALISM
Until the beginning of the nineteenth century, the genres of composition and the formal models developed in Italy, France, and German areas were reproduced all over Europe. However, particularly during the second half of the century, there was a rediscovery of folk music in such countries as Russia, Bohemia, and the Scandinavian regions. Their chosen medium was the opera and the symphonic poem, because it was possible to write librettos in local idioms and select topics and characters from national literature and history. The term "national schools" for this phenomenon is not actually appropriate, as it assumes a stylistic continuity from teacher to pupil that, in reality, does not exist. Above, Bedřich Smetana, father of Bohemian music.

NOVEMBER 1830: WARSAW ROSE UP
The Arsenal and the palace of the Grand Duke Constantine, brother of the Czar, were attacked. Constantine escaped and the town fell into the hands of rebels. Poland regained its independence.

THE MILITARY AND THE ARISTOCRACY
First, General Clopicki, who fought with Napoleon, then Prince Mikhail Radziwill were chosen to rule Poland. After a long siege, in September 1831, Warsaw again fell to Russia.

♦ THE REBELS
Students, members of the middle class, and veterans of the Russia campaign of 1812, when Poland was Napoleon's ally, supported the military. Many were forced to leave the country.

♦ **Secret societies**
Modeled after the more ancient Masons, secret societies developed in backward countries. Many future liberal leaders were members of these societies.

♦ **1848**
Two important subversive forces undermined the European political system: the patriotic movements and the more advanced democratic and socialist movements. The first ones aimed at creating a national state in such politically disjointed nations as Italy, Germany, Poland, and Hungary. The second forces claimed equality among citizens, popular sovereignty, and universal suffrage. This turbulent situation exploded in 1848, when Europe went through a violent revolutionary wave. In France, the king was dethroned and the Republic was proclaimed. Vienna, Berlin, and Germany rose up and anti-Austrian outbreaks burst out in Hungary, Bohemia, Croatia, and Italy. Karl Marx (above) and Friedrich Engels wrote the *Communist Manifesto*, the guide of the emerging workers' movement.

♦ **The Polish flag**
Rebels waved the red and white Polish flag to proclaim their national identity.

For every European nation the flag became the symbol of national ideals.

3. Chopin's life ♦ *In 1827 Chopin's sister Emilia, barely fourteen, died of tuberculosis. In 1828 he went to Berlin, and the following year he listened in awe to Paganini in Warsaw. Graduated from the Lycée, he went to Vienna, where he met Czerny, Schuppanzigh, and the publisher, Haslinger. In 1830 he decided to leave Poland, and on November 2 he left Warsaw. He would never see it again. The news of the Warsaw riots took him completely by surprise in Vienna.* ➻

Musical amateurs

Playing for their own pleasure at home, a popular old custom among aristocrats became fashionable at the beginning of the nineteenth century, even among rich bankers such as the Mendelssohns and the Itzigs in Berlin, and military officers, professionals, and artisans. The reason for this popularity was the versatility of the piano, which could be conveniently used for solo playing, for singing and instrumental accompaniment, or as a first orchestral element for two and four hands. In Europe, and especially in England, France, and the German-speaking areas, where the number of middle class citizens was increasing, there was an extraordinary growth in piano production, private lessons, and musical publishing companies.

Music at home
Hausmusik (House Music) is the German term for playing music at home and writing music for home entertainment. Literally, it means "domestic music."

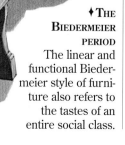

♦The Biedermeier period
The linear and functional Biedermeier style of furniture also refers to the tastes of an entire social class.

♦Two, four, and six hands
Piano arrangements play an important role in performing operas and symphonies.

♦ **CLIMBING THE SOCIAL LADDER**
The study of singing and piano, once only performed by the aristocracy, became a requirement in the education of wealthy young ladies.

♦ **THE REBIRTH OF CHORAL MUSIC**
City choral societies and important choral festivals answered the demands of German and English amateur musicians.

♦ **A MASS MARKET REPERTOIRE**
The growing number of amateur musicians contributed to the birth of light, easy, and sentimental piano music. The most famous example is *The Maiden's Prayer* by the Polish composer Thekla Badarzewska, which in 1864 alone was reprinted over seven times. The melodies were also adapted for various instruments and instrumental groups, as the amateurs were not only pianists. In less than forty years, more than fifty versions of Gounod's (above) *Ave Maria* came onto the market. To increase the sales, publishers did not hesitate to give fantastic names to some of the great composers' works. In 1841 Chopin complained about the London publisher Wessel for turning his *First Scherzo*, op. 20 into *Le Banquet Infernal*, and publishing some nocturnes under the colorful names of *Les Murmures de la Seine*, *Les Zéphirs*, *Les Plaintives*, and *Les Soupirs*.

♦ **THE PIANO**
The piano became the king of musical instruments, especially in its more economic and less bulky versions: the upright and table models.

♦ **INSTRUMENTAL COMBINATIONS**
To reach a broader public, successful pieces were adapted for various instruments and ensembles.

THE ROMANTIC *LIED*

The German word *Lied* (song) [plural form: *Lieder*] stands for poetry in music. This typically German musical genre flourished during the romantic era either in the multivoice forms, popularly used by choral societies and amateur musicians, or in beautiful pieces for solo voice with piano accompaniment. With its power to express the innermost part of the artist's soul by connecting words to sounds, the *Lied* for solo voice became the major genre of German romanticism. In a *Lied*, the melody can remain the same verse after verse—strophic *Lied*—or it can change for every verse—modified strophic *Lied*.

♦ SCHUMANN: TORMENTED GENIUS
Cultivated by Mendelssohn and Weber, who developed a successful genre for piano music, *Lied ohne Worte* (Songs without words), the romantic *Lied* reached its height because of Robert Schumann (1810–1856). In his almost 250 *Lieder*, Schumann was able to overlap life and art, which is so common in romanticism. In 1840, the year he finally married Clara Wieck (above), he wrote almost 120 *Lieder*, mostly devoted to love. Among them are his major masterpieces such as the cycles *Frauenliebe und Leben*, op. 42, (*Woman's Love and Life*) to the text by Adalbert von Chamisso, and *Dichterliebe*, op. 48 (*Poet's Love*) to the text by Heinrich Heine. After Schumann's death the great *Lieder* continued with Johannes Brahms (1833–1897) and Hugo Wolf (1860–1903).

THE WINTER VOYAGE
This is the title of a remarkable and yearning cycle of 24 *Lieder* written by the thirty-year-old Schubert in 1827, one year before he died. Its music portrays the frozen and barren atmosphere found in the verses of the German poet Wilhelm Müller (1794–1827).

♦ THE PILGRIM
A typical character of German romanticism, the pilgrim was the protagonist of another famous *Lied* by Schubert.

♦ **THE FATHER OF THE ROMANTIC *LIED***
The Viennese Franz Peter Schubert (1797–1828) composed about six hundred *Lieder* as well as symphonies, quartets, and sonatas for piano. Overlooked by his contemporaries, he was discovered and admired by the romantics.

♦ **WINTER DESOLATION**
In this work, inner desperation is mirrored by nature. It is a very cold night, the wind blows sharply, and the ground is frozen.

♦ **THE COUNTRY CEMETERY**
Jack-o'-lanterns, an owl, and crows make up the funereal symbols the romantics liked to use.

FRENCH ROMANTICISM

During the first half of the nineteenth century, a stream of new ideas invaded French cultural life. Groups of young intellectuals gathered around such celebrities as the writer Victor Hugo. They were the men of letters, painters, and sculptors of *Jeune France* (Young France), who repudiated the rigid rules of classical art. In the preface to his drama *Cromwell* (1827), Hugo pointed to Shakespeare and Schiller as the new models to follow. He proposed smoother verses, condemned the old rules of time, place, and action of Aristotle, and found in history the source of modern drama. On February 25, 1830, strong reactions from audiences and the media followed the première of Hugo's drama *Hernani* at the Comédie Française. French literary romanticism, more sentimental and whimsical than any other, as a reaction also to the rationalism of the Enlightenment, had found its style.

♦ SHAKESPEARE AS A LEGEND
"It was the first time that I saw in the theater true passions exciting real men and women," commented Alexandre Dumas during the 1827 performances of the dramas by Shakespeare (above). He considered Shakespeare "the man who has created more after God." Many romantic musicians were inspired by him: Berlioz wrote the *Fantastic Symphony* in 1830, *King Lear's Overture* in 1831, the dramatic symphony *Romeo and Juliet* in 1839, and the opera *Beatrice and Benedict* in 1862, adapted from *Much Ado about Nothing*. In 1826 Mendelssohn composed the overture to *A Midsummer Night's Dream*, and other pieces in 1843. Wagner wrote *Liebesverbot* from *Measure for Measure*, Schumann the overture for *Julius Caesar* in 1851, and Liszt, the symphonic poem, *Hamlet* in 1858.

♦ OPHELIA
Berlioz fell desperately in love with Harriet Smithson, a mediocre actress, without ever having met her.

♦ DE VIGNY
In 1827 Alfred de Vigny (1797–1863) left the army to write. In 1829 he translated Shakespeare's *Othello* into French.

HAMLET IN PARIS
September 1827: At the Odéon Theatre Charles Kemble's theater company presented Shakespeare in English. For the French audiences, it was a striking revelation.

♦ **VICTOR HUGO** (1802–1885) Beyond its ideological relevance, the theater did not represent the best of Hugo's literary work.

♦ **GÉRARD DE NERVAL** Born in 1808, he published at twenty a translation of Goethe's *Faust* that the author admired. Eventually, he went mad and killed himself in 1855.

♦ **BERLIOZ** At twenty-four, he was enamored of Shakespeare's works, although he did not understand English, and of Miss Smithson, whom he married five years later.

♦ **CHATEAUBRIAND'S INFLUENCE** In his book *René*, published in 1805, François-René de Chateaubriand (1768–1848) expressed the feelings of an entire generation, that everything in life is senseless, empty, inconsistent, and dull. According to this new "*mal du siècle*," there is no remedy except in isolation or suicide, or by performing extraordinary feats that would make one's life into something wonderful.

♦ **EUGÈNE DELACROIX** (1798–1863) Delacroix is considered the father of romantic painters, but without the frenzy of Nerval.

PAGANINI

A symbol of unmatched virtuosity, Niccolò Paganini began his triumphant career in Europe when he was fifty, during the period 1828 to 1834. He lived a dissolute life, and had many passionate love affairs that caused him pain as well as forcing him to spend some time in jail. Although his compositions are not always tasteful nor always artistically superior, his compositions, especially his *24 Caprices* op. 1, show an extraordinary talent in violin playing. Paganini is the true prototype of the romantic virtuoso who inspired an entire generation to emulate his ability and virtuosity on the keyboard.

♦ PAGANINI'S GREATEST FANS
Around 1830 Paganini (above, in a caricature) had a strong influence on piano music. Inspired by his *24 Caprices* for solo violin, Chopin conceived the *Études*, op. 10 and op. 25. These works reached and then surpassed the technical standards of the time. Liszt also was attracted by Paganini's charisma. In 1832, after listening to him, Liszt composed not only the *Grande Fantaisie de Bravoure sur la Clochette*, source of the *Grandes Études de Paganini*, but he made great changes in his style of piano writing. In 1839 Schumann credited Paganini with having pushed Liszt to his limits. In 1830 it was Schumann's turn to emulate the illustrious model with his *Études after Caprices by Paganini*, op. 3 and op. 10.

A PACT WITH THE DEVIL?
Many of his contemporaries believed that Paganini's virtuosity was due to a pact he had made with the devil. When he died in Nice, in 1840, the bishop refused to bury him in consecrated ground.

♦ A DIZZYING SCHEDULE
He was born in Genoa in 1782. Between 1828 and 1834 he played all over Europe. In one year alone, he performed 151 concerts in France and England, traveling almost 62,000 miles (10,000 km).

♦ BRAVO!
During Paganini's concert tours, many great musicians, including Schubert, Chopin, Mendelssohn, Schumann, Liszt, and Berlioz, applauded him.

♦ ROMANTIC DEDICATIONS
In 1838 Paganini (above, in a miniature) gave 20,000 French francs to Berlioz, who was having great financial problems. Berlioz paid him back by dedicating his *Romeo and Juliet* to him. The romantics often exchanged dedications. Sometimes, it was an even exchange, as in the case of Schumann's dedication to Chopin of the *Kreisleriana* or the *C-Major Fantasy*, op. 17, to Liszt. In return, he acknowledged Chopin's *Second Ballade* and Liszt's *Sonata in B Minor*. At other times, it was not so equal; for instance, Chopin dedicated his *12 Études*, op. 10 to Liszt, who replied with the *Grande Fantaisie sur la Fiancée* by Auber, a minor work. There was also a literary interchange. Mendelssohn dedicated his *Third Quartet* to Goethe, and Schumann did the same with his *Dances of the David-leaguers*, op. 6.

♦ SHOWMANSHIP
Paganini was a showman who reproduced animal sounds with his violin, improvised on one string, and wore glasses with colored lenses on stage.

PARIS

♦ **MUSIC CAPITAL**
The Paris of the 1820s and 1830s hosted quality music and a number of great composers including the Italian Gioachino Rossini (portrait above), Luigi Cherubini, director of the Conservatory, and Ferdinando Paër, head of the *Théâtre des Italiens*. The most acclaimed pianists of the time performed in Paris, such as Franz Liszt, Friedrich Wilhelm Kalkbrenner, Henri Herz, Ferdinand Hiller, and Johann Peter Pixis. Composers such as Liszt and Berlioz contributed witty articles to music publications such as the *Revue Musical*, headed by its chief critic, François-Joseph Fétis.

The elegant aristocracy, the entrepreneurial middle class, and the poor arrived in Paris from rural areas in search of their fortunes. They did not coexist without some tensions, however. In this explosive climate, the reactionary politics of Charles X succeeded in igniting the July Revolution, which, in 1830 resulted in the victory of the constitutional-liberal system and established the political power in the hands of the middle class (or *bourgeoisie*). During the next two years, this example was also seen in Belgium and in England, where industrialization had become even stronger. In the decades to come, in all countries, the principal social and political issue was the confrontation between the middle class and the emerging industrial and urban working class, which was beginning to demand better living conditions and recognition of its political rights.

SCENES OF LIFE IN PARIS
Arriving in Paris in 1831, Chopin wrote, "One sees here, at the same time, great luxury and the most extreme poverty, the highest virtues and the lowest forms of depravity." This was a result of the city's rapid demographic development.

♦ **POPULAR THEATERS**
Around the mid-1830s, there were a dozen minor theaters in Paris with small orchestras staging popular musical shows.

THÉÂTRE DE L'ATELIER RUE D'ORSEL

4. CHOPIN'S LIFE ♦ *Leaving Vienna in July 1831, Chopin arrived in Paris in September, where he met Kalkbrenner. He did not want to study with Kalkbrenner, but the two remained friends. In Germany, Schumann published an enthusiastic review of Chopin's* Variations, *op. 2. On February 26, 1832 Chopin premièred at the Salle Pleyel with Kalkbrenner, Mendelssohn, and Ferdinand Hiller. His request for an audition at the* Société des Concerts du Conservatoire *was rejected, and a period of financial problems began.* ➤

THE FANTASTIC SYMPHONY

On December 5, 1830, at the Paris Conservatory, François-Antoine Habeneck directed the first performance of *The Fantastic Symphony*, op. 14 by Hector Berlioz. Aside from the established German symphonic tradition, the young Frenchman created a superb orchestral structure, articulated in five movements with a recurrent theme. A literary program with strong autobiographical elements—a perfect example of a romantic combination of life and art—permeates this work. The expressive but long and irregular melody of the beginning returns, transfigured repeatedly in the subsequent movements. It is the *idée fixe* (fixed idea) and represents the woman he loved, the actress Harriet Smithson.

♦ **BERLIOZ: A MAN OF PASSION**
Born in 1803 in France, he studied flute and guitar; he was the only romantic who did not play the piano. In Paris he studied composition with Jean-François Lesueur, and counterpoint and fugue with Anton Reicha. In 1831, failing to win the love of Harriet Smithson, he turned to the young pianist, Camille Moke (above). Meanwhile, he composed the *Fantastic Symphony*, in which he expressed his love for Harriet. When he discovered that his fiancée had left him for Camille Pleyel, he decided to kill the two lovers, her mother, and himself; however, he would never carry it out. This shocking experience produced *Lélio or Le Rétour à la Vie*, a sequel to the *Fantastic*. Finally, he met Harriet Smithson again and married her in October 1833.

EPISODES IN THE LIFE OF AN ARTIST
This is the symphony's subtitle. The program, distributed at the première, described the work as similar to "the spoken text of an opera."

♦ ***A BALL***
In the second movement, the vision of his beloved troubles the artist in the midst of a crowded ball.

♦ ***DREAMS AND PASSIONS***
The first movement describes various feelings such as love, tenderness, jealousy, and rage, inspired by the vision of the woman he loved.

♦ **HECTOR BERLIOZ AND HARRIET SMITHSON.**

♦ **THE TREATISE ON INSTRUMENTATION**
In 1843 Berlioz (left, in a caricature) published this brilliant work on the best way to use musical instruments.

♦ **SCENE IN THE FIELDS**
In the third movement, the young man flees to the countryside to escape his anguish.

♦ **MARCH TO THE GALLOWS**
In the fourth movement, the young man is sure of his beloved's betrayal and poisons himself with opium. He dreams that he has killed her and witnesses his own execution.

♦ **SABBATH NIGHT'S DREAM**
In the fifth movement, his nightmares have become more vivid and he is at a witches' Sabbath where a parody of the *Dies Irae* echoes.

THE PARIS OPÉRA

Since the seventeenth century, French opera had appeared at Paris' main lyrical theater following a model that contained scenic elements, dance, and choruses. Around 1830 a new type of opera, which also used this model, as well as works by Spontini and Cherubini, appeared. It was spectacular, characterized by sumptuous scenery and choreography, the extensive use of chorus and orchestra, and great singers. Operas such as Auber's *La Muette de Portici* (1828), Rossini's *William Tell* (1829), and Meyerbeer's *Robert le Diable* (1831) defined what was called *grand opéra*. Its most important representative was the German Giacomo Meyerbeer (1791–1864), who also wrote *The Huguenots*, *The Prophet*, and *The African Maid*.

✦ THE VARIED VIEWS OF ROMANTICS

The operas by Meyerbeer (above) generated contrasting opinions among romantics. Chopin thought that *Robert le Diable* was "a masterpiece of the new school." On the other hand, Mendelssohn believed that "compared to a work of art it is like a pictorial decoration to a painting: The decoration is certainly effective, but at a closer look, one knows that it is painted with feet." *The Huguenots* was compared to an encyclopedia by Berlioz, and was a source of disgust for Schumann, who reviewed *The Prophet* by drawing a cross. Even Wagner was merciless. When he was young, Wagner admired Meyerbeer, but now saw in his music "effects without causes." Apparently, German composers did not forgive their colleagues and fellow countrymen for betraying the German cause.

✦ ROMANTICS AND THE MIDDLE AGES

The action takes place in Palermo, Sicily, and the literary Middle Ages (thirteenth century). The finale culminates in Palermo's Gothic cathedral.

✦ DEVILS AND NUNS

Opera is rich in such Gothic elements as the dance of the nuns rising out of graves.

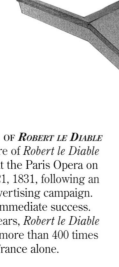

THE TRIUMPH OF *ROBERT LE DIABLE*
The première of *Robert le Diable* took place at the Paris Opera on November 21, 1831, following an intense advertising campaign. It was an immediate success. For thirty years, *Robert le Diable* was staged more than 400 times in France alone.

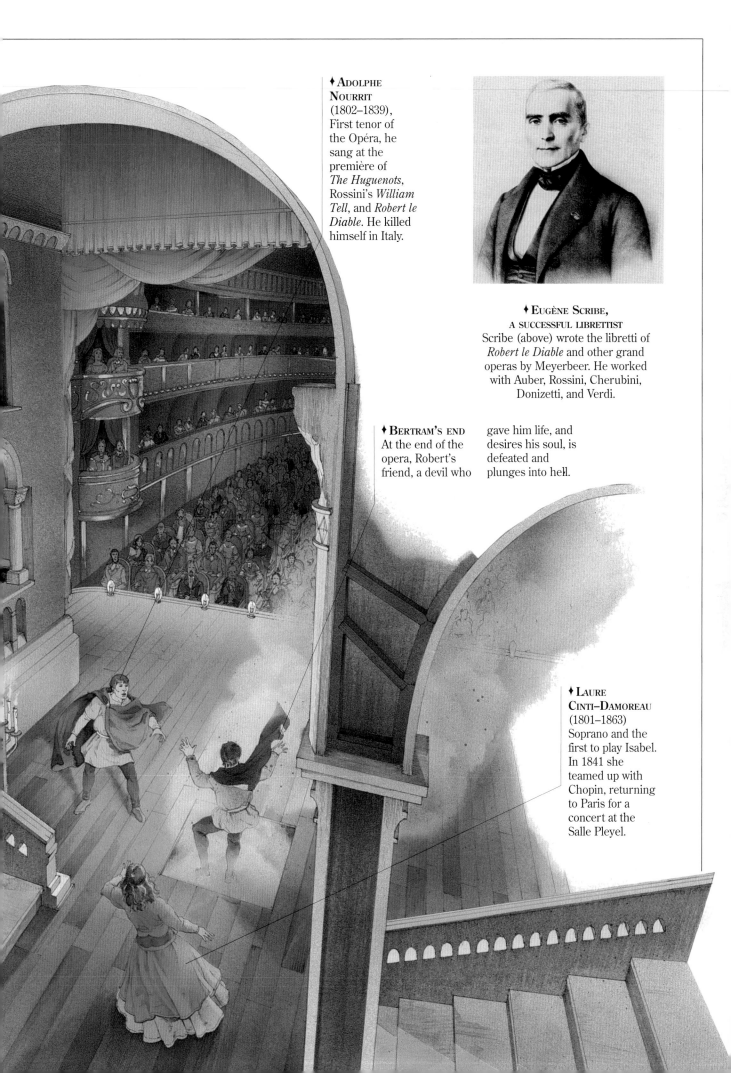

♦ **ADOLPHE NOURRIT** (1802–1839), First tenor of the Opéra, he sang at the première of *The Huguenots*, Rossini's *William Tell*, and *Robert le Diable*. He killed himself in Italy.

♦ **EUGÈNE SCRIBE, A SUCCESSFUL LIBRETTIST**
Scribe (above) wrote the libretti of *Robert le Diable* and other grand operas by Meyerbeer. He worked with Auber, Rossini, Cherubini, Donizetti, and Verdi.

♦ **BERTRAM'S END**
At the end of the opera, Robert's friend, a devil who gave him life, and desires his soul, is defeated and plunges into hell.

♦ **LAURE CINTI–DAMOREAU** (1801–1863) Soprano and the first to play Isabel. In 1841 she teamed up with Chopin, returning to Paris for a concert at the Salle Pleyel.

THE ROMANTIC SYMPHONY

The works of Mendelssohn and Schuman show that the symphony was a problem for German romantics. At one end, tastes shifted toward shorter and more supple forms of music or toward program music. At the other, Beethoven stands out as a greatly admired but unattainable model. Mendelssohn published only three of his five symphonies; however, one of them is not considered a true symphony because it contains many sections that are sung, and the other two are derived from an extra-musical motif. Schumann's situation was the same. He debuted at thirty-one with a symphony inspired by a poem on springtime. Twelve years later, he rewrote the *Second* in a cyclic form, after he had already finished the *Second* and the *Third*, known as the *"Rhenish"* in five movements.

1831, GULF OF NAPLES: MENDELSSOHN WRITES THE *"ITALIAN"*
Begun during his trip to Italy in 1833, and performed for the first time in London, the *Italian* was revised several times by its composer, in spite of its success. It was published posthumously as *Symphony no. 4*.

♦ **PROGRAM MUSIC**
Outside Germany, the symphony had a different fate. Chopin never wrote symphonies; he composed music only for piano and used the orchestra only in his early compositions for piano and orchestra. Berlioz, with his *Fantastic Symphony*, composed a masterpiece that was not in the German tradition. Even Liszt wrote program music. After beginning a *Revolutionary Symphony* in Paris, in 1854 and 1856, he composed the *Faust Symphony*, based on Goethe's *Faust*. It is in three movements and deals with the three main characters of the drama (above, *Faust with Marguerite in Prison*, a lithograph by Delacroix). He also composed the *Dante Symphony*, based on Dante's *Divine Comedy*. It has only two movements: *Inferno* and *Purgatory*.

♦ **THE BEAUTY OF ITALY**
Mendelssohn was fascinated by the smells and sea of Italy, described by Goethe as "the land where lemons blossom."

Mendelssohn also worked on the *Scotch Symphony* and the *First Walpurgis Night*, based on Goethe's text. He regarded Italy with admiration, but the musical level of Italian orchestras, choruses, and theaters, strongly criticized in his letters, disappointed him.

♦ WATERCOLORS
Mendelssohn was a gifted landscape artist. His delicate watercolors reproduced some of the most charming scenes he admired during his journey.

♦ SCHUBERT, THE ISOLATED COMPOSER
Franz Schubert (above) died at thirty-one in 1828, before any of his symphonies were performed or published. After composing six symphonies when he was young, he finally wrote the *Symphony in C Major* in 1825–1826, performed for the first time in 1839. *The Symphony in B Minor* was called *The Unfinished Symphony* because Schubert, in 1822, finished only the first two movements. It was rediscovered in 1865. In these two masterpieces, although apparently following tradition, Schubert shows his complete independence from Beethoven (who was already recognized by Schumann). The dreamlike themes, the lighthearted freedom of passing from one tonality to another, and the actual musical structure prove this. In so doing, he established a model for late-romantic era composers such as Anton Bruckner and Gustav Mahler.

♦ THE SALTARELLO
The last movement of Mendelssohn's *Symphony no. 4* is a saltarello, a lively dance that pays homage to Italian folklore.

Private salons

In Europe, appearances at the salons of aristocrats, government officials, and wealthy businessmen were important for the future of an artist. In his writings in 1836, Schumann distinguished between the salons of the well-to-do and those of the intellectuals. The music played for the first group, called "salon music," had to be enjoyable, light, and sentimental. On the other hand, the music performed in intellectual circles, as at the Mendelssohns' or at the mansion of the Parisian banker, Auguste Léo, where Chopin was at home, was less popular. Ignaz Moscheles played the latest and most recently published Beethoven sonatas at Auguste Léo's home. These sonatas would remain incomprehensible to many and were neglected for a long time.

♦ **CLARA WIECK**
(1819–1896)
Clara Wieck's father, Friedrich, taught her the piano. She made her first public appearance at the age of eight, even showing her ability as a composer. At twelve she began a tour that brought her to Weimar, where she played for the octogenarian Goethe, and to Paris. In 1838 the Emperor awarded her the title of "chamber virtuoso." Against her father's wishes, she became engaged to Robert Schumann, whom she married in 1840. Mother of eight, she continued to perform throughout Europe, even after her husband's death in 1856, when she developed a strong friendship with Johannes Brahms. From 1878 to 1892 she taught at the Frankfurt Conservatory. Her repertoire contained works by Schumann, Beethoven (including his last sonatas), Mendelssohn, Chopin, and Brahms.

MARCH 1832: CLARA WIECK IN PARIS
The twelve-year-old Clara Wieck, a child prodigy from Leipzig, played the piano in the Paris salon of Princess Vandamore in the presence of ambassadors, government officials, princes, and the pianist Kalkbrenner.

♦ **THE ANDALUSIAN GUITARIST**
Clara had to share the attention with a fiery Andalusian guitarist in native costume, a touch of glamour typical of the Paris salons.

5. CHOPIN'S LIFE ♦ *Thanks to Polish aristocratic refugees in Paris, he became the most popular piano teacher in town. In the spring of 1843 he went to Germany where he met Mendelssohn. In December he played in a concert directed by Berlioz, and in 1835 he performed at the* Théâtre des Italiens *and debuted at the* Société des Concerts du Conservatoire. *In the summer he went to Karlsbad, where he saw his parents for the last time. Upon the invitation of the Wodzinskis, he traveled to Dresden. Later, he arrived in Leipzig, where he again saw Mendelssohn and met Robert Schumann and Friedrich and Clara Wieck.* ➡➔

♦ **IN THE GOOD GRACES OF THE ARISTOCRACY**
To be welcomed into exclusive aristocratic Parisian circles meant a wealth of private lessons and access to large concert halls.

♦ **FRIEDRICH WIECK**
(1785–1873)
After opening up a piano factory, he decided to teach. His students included his daughter Clara, Schumann, and Hans von Bülow.

♦ **A LOST OPPORTUNITY**
On April 9 Clara was to debut in a renowned Parisian concert hall; however, a cholera outburst in Paris forced the Wiecks to quickly return to Leipzig.

♦ **FRIEDRICH WILHELM KALKBRENNER**
Born in Germany in 1785, he studied in Paris and Vienna, where he met Haydn and Beethoven. In Paris, he was Pleyel's partner and a highly regarded piano teacher.

SCHUMANN

Like Mendelssohn, Schumann had a strong literary and philosophy background. Until his twenties, he alternated between music and literature. He was complex and tormented, but a highly creative figure whose constant overlapping of art and life perfectly embodied the prototype of the romantic musician described by Hoffmann and other writers. Amazingly enough, he stated that he had learned more about counterpoint from reading Jean Paul's novels than from his music composition teacher. The fact that he was recognized more as a literary critic than as a musician, the universal fame of his wife Clara, and his depression and instability added to his anguish. In 1854, after an attempted suicide in the Rhine, he was confined in a mental institution where he died two years later.

♦ **PERIODS IN SCHUMANN'S LIFE**
For almost ten years, the German Robert Schumann (above, in a portrait) (1810–1856) was absorbed by the piano. All his compositions until op. 23 are only for piano. Then, he lost interest in the piano and gradually developed new interests. In 1840 he turned to the *Lied*, writing a record number of more than 120. In 1841 he took up symphonic music. He composed two symphonies (the *First Symphony* and an early version of what would become the *Fourth*—and last—*Symphony* ten years later), and the first movement of his only *Concerto* for piano and orchestra. In 1842 he discovered chamber music and composed the *String Quartet*, op. 41, the *Piano Quintet*, op. 44, and the *Piano Quartet*, op. 47. At the same time, he worked on an opera, and between 1847 and 1850 he finished *Genoveva*, his only great work in the genre.

"LITTLE SCENES COMPOSED FOR THE PIANO IN FOUR NOTES"
Carnival, op. 9 is centered on the four notes present in the German word *Asch*, the name of the town of the girl he had fallen in love with. These are also the only letters in his name that are capable of being translated into musical notes.

♦ **EUSEBIUS**
Protagonist of the fifth piece of *Carnival*, Eusebius represents the contemplative side of Schumann's personality.

♦ **FAREWELL TO THE PIANO**
After injuring himself with a device intended to strengthen the fourth finger of his right hand, Schumann's career as a pianist came to an end.

♦ THE PROTAGONISTS
OF *CARNIVAL*
Among the
characters
portrayed in
Carnival's twenty-
one sketches are
Clara Wieck,
Chopin, and
Paganini.

♦ A PHENOMENAL
MUSICAL CRITIC
In 1831
Schumann
reviewed
Variations, op. 2
by Chopin, who
was still unknown
at the time.
He said
enthusiastically
of them, "Hats off,
gentlemen—a
genius!" In 1834,
in Leipzig, he
published a
musical journal
whose articles
were signed by
the members of a
fictitious "David's
League" at war
with the
"Philistines" of
music: "Eusebius"
and "Florestan,"
the polar
divisions of his
own ego, or
"Master Raro,"
the wise side.
In "Master Raro,"
inspired by the
figure of
Friedrich Wieck,
extremes were
balanced out.
In 1853, before
he went mad,
he wrote an
article entitled
"New Roads"
to announce a
new talent to the
world, the
twenty-year-old
Johannes Brahms
(above in a
photograph).

♦ FLORESTAN
Described in the
sixth piece, he is
the opposite of
Eusebius. He
represents the
most tempestuous
side of
Schumann's
personality.

37

THE PIANO RECITAL

At the beginning of the nineteenth century, performances by pianists who presented their own compositions took place in a concert that was a combined effort with singers, other instrumentalists, and chamber groups. The solo concert, as a musical evening led by a solo pianist who played mostly other composers' music, did not yet exist. It was Ignaz Moscheles who invented the recital. In 1837, in London, he gave a piano concert (with only an intermezzo of four short vocal pieces) by playing mainly the works of past composers. Two years later, in Rome, Liszt presented his "musical soliloquies," which were concerts of his own compositions. The term *recital* was coined in 1840 during one of his concerts in London.

♦ **IGNAZ MOSCHELES** (1794–1870) Mendelssohn's friend and teacher and highly esteemed by Chopin, Moscheles stopped performing in concerts by 1840.

FEBRUARY 1837: MOSCHELES' CHALLENGE
Moscheles chose "history" (Bach, Händel, and Scarlatti) and his close contemporaries, Beethoven and Weber. He presented only a few of his *Études*.

THE SCORE
Generally, musicians followed a score. Clara Wieck was among the first to play from memory.

♦ **THE REDISCOVERY OF THE PAST**
To perform Scarlatti, Moscheles used the harpsichord, an instrument that was no longer being used at that time.

♦ **A PERPLEXED AUDIENCE**
Not everyone appreciated this less sparkling evening, one without such fashionable pieces as fantasies on opera themes.

LISZT

Born in Hungary in 1811, Liszt was a child prodigy. He completed his training in Vienna and Paris. Famous in Europe at fourteen, he almost quit his concert career at sixteen. At eighteen, he considered becoming a priest, but in his early thirties, inspired by the great example of Paganini, he returned to the musical scene. Courtly, idolized by women, and greatly admired by the public, Liszt soon became a foremost piano virtuoso. His fame, however, would hurt him, obscuring his great importance as a composer and musical interpreter. The contrast between his lighthearted love affairs and his deep mysticism is striking. By his own definition, he was "half gypsy and half Franciscan."

♦ **TRANSCENDENTAL VIRTUOSITY**
Originally meant as a short composition based on a single technical difficulty, the étude was transformed by romantics into a work of art. In 1833 Chopin published his *12 Études*, op. 10, and in 1837, his *12 Études*, op. 25. Liszt (above), already a composer at fifteen of 12 études, completely revised them in 1837 and again in 1851. At the latter date, he added an adjective to the title, as well as to the title of the six *Grandes Études de Paganini* that would mark romantic virtuosity, that of transcendental. As for Schumann, after his *Studies for the Piano Arranged from Paganini's Caprices*, he composed the *Symphonic Études for Piano*, op. 13, (1834–1835), whose title emphasizes its complex writing. Schumann achieved a complex formality through an original fusion between the form of the étude and that of the variation.

♦ **"LISZTOMANIA" IN EUROPE**
Heine called Liszt's virtuoso performances "Lisztomania." It culminated in the years 1839 to 1847, when he played in 166 towns in eighteen different countries, from Portugal to Russia, and from Denmark to Turkey.

♦ A CHARITY GALA
The entrance ticket for the gala organized to support Italian refugees cost 40 francs.

1837: THE PIANO DUEL BETWEEN LISZT AND THALBERG
Organized in Cristina Belgioioso's Paris salon to resolve some questions raised by the media, the duel did not have a decisive winner. The audience is said to have commented: "Thalberg is certainly the first pianist in the world, but Liszt is the only one."

♦ SIGISMUND THALBERG
(1812–1871) Thalberg was famous for the songlike quality of his work and for his clever use of the pedal.

♦ THE PROGRAM
Liszt played his *Divertissement sur la cavatine 'I tuoi frequenti palpiti'* from Pacini's *Niobe*, and Thalberg, his *Fantasy on Moses in Egypt* by Rossini.

♦ BEYOND VIRTUOSITY
Liszt (above) lived almost forty years longer than Mendelssohn and Chopin and thirty more than Schumann. During that period, there were many changes in his life. In 1848 he abandoned his piano career and accepted a position as a musical director and conductor in Weimar. Here, he composed his symphonic poems while working as an orchestra director generously promoting, among others, the music of Wagner, Berlioz, and Smetana. He was also a piano teacher, training many excellent pianists who spread his teaching theories across Europe. From 1861 to 1869 he lived in Rome, where he devoted himself to sacred music, and in 1865 he received the tonsure and minor orders. During his last years, his music and, in particular, a series of short piano pieces, renounced any piano virtuosity in favor of a bold writing form using harmony and tone color.

♦ CRISTINA BELGIOIOSO
Her Parisian salon hosted intellectuals from all over Europe. Born in Milan in 1808, she played an important role in the Italian "Risorgimento" (Renaissance).

6. CHOPIN'S LIFE ♦ *In the summer of 1836, in Marienbad, he declared his love to Maria Wodzinska, who accepted his courtship only if her parents approved. In Paris Liszt introduced him to the writer George Sand, and in the spring of 1837, his correspondence with Maria ended. Chopin gathered up all the letters and one rose in a package on which he wrote "my unhappiness." George Sand invited him to her home in Nohant, but Chopin went with Camille Pleyel to London, where he played in Broadwood's concert hall.* ➠

GEORGE SAND

Chopin's most significant love affair was with the writer George Sand (1804–1876). It lasted from 1838 to 1847. The choice of a male name as a pseudonym—her real name was Aurore Dupin de Francueil—was one of her many nonconformist and defiant attitudes. She settled in Paris with her two children from her broken marriage with Baron Dudevant. She often wore male suits, smoked big cigars, was part of artists' circles, and had a series of turbulent love affairs. Her personality contrasted with that of the delicate and sensitive Chopin. A prolific author of successful novels, today largely forgotten, her *Complete Works*, published in the second half of the nineteenth century, are compiled in 109 volumes.

IN THE NAME OF FRIENDSHIP
Chopin and George Sand visited the Parisian studio of the painter Eugène Delacroix. As a favor, the painter gave some art lessons to Maurice, the writer's son.

♦ **TUBERCULOSIS**
This infectious and chronic illness affects the lungs. In its early stages, it presents very vague symptoms, but later, a recurrent cough appears accompanied by hemoptysis (coughing up of blood). Recognized for a long time, it appeared again at the beginning of the nineteenth century, due in large part to poor hygiene. In England, between 1851 and 1860, the average mortality rate was 3,480 cases for every million inhabitants, and in Belgium it was 3,560 cases. It was called the "white plague." Its victims included Weber, Chopin, his sister Emilia, his friend Matuszynski, Novalis, one brother and his fiancée, one of Liszt's children, and two of Schumann's children. The TBC bacillus was discovered in 1882 by Robert Koch (above, in a photo).

♦ **DELACROIX**
Born in 1798, cultivated, and never satisfied, Delacroix was a good friend of Chopin's. He refused the label of "romantic" for his art, but he is considered today the most representative French romantic painter.

♦ **MAURICE DUDEVANT**
Chopin never had a good relationship with Dudevant, but his affection for Maurice's sister, Solange, lasted his entire life.

♦ **PAINTING AND MUSIC**
Delacroix believed that painting should be as festive to the eyes as music is to the ears.

♦ **THE ROMANTIC POINT OF VIEW**
A modern composer for his time, Chopin (above, in the portrait by Delacroix) actually had no modern tastes and appreciated few of his contemporaries. He neither understood the paintings of his friend Delacroix, who considered Chopin second only to Mozart, nor Schumann's music. Even Schumann, one of his longtime admirers, was bewildered by some of Chopin's choices. Liszt believed that Chopin's last compositions were the product of a "sick sensibility." Another amazing case of incomprehension among romantics, besides the attitude toward Meyerbeer, is that of Mendelssohn toward the *Fantastic.* He wrote, "Here and there all the instruments have moments of nausea and vomit music that makes the listener very sad."

♦ **A PORTRAIT SPLIT IN HALF**
Delacroix portrayed Chopin and George Sand together. The painting is physically split into two halves. One half hangs in the Louvre, and the other in Copenhagen.

7. CHOPIN'S LIFE ♦ *On February 25, 1838, Chopin gave a private performance for King Louis-Philippe. On March 12, in Rouen, he played with an orchestra for the last time. In June his affair with George Sand began, and in October he followed the writer and her two children to Majorca, whose mild climate he hoped would cure him. However, the trip was terrible for his health and after four months, the couple returned to France. Chopin was unable to reach Paris so they remained in Marseilles until May, when they went to Nohant. On October 29, 1839, he again played for the king, together with Moscheles.* ⟫→

NOCTURNES

In the early nineteenth century, amateurs favored romantic pieces for piano and voice and generated forms that brought the keyboard back to the simple and symmetrical structure of a chanson (A-B-A'), performed with a dreamy melody using the right hand and arpeggios using the left. The improvement of the right, the "loud" pedal, contributed to a richer and wider range of sounds. The first works of this genre, published around 1812 by John Field, soon afterward were called "Romances." Field adopted the French title *Nocturnes* and achieved European fame. Following the example of Field and Maria Szymanowska, Chopin composed his first *Nocturne* in 1827. He would write nocturnes all his life, perfecting a genre that has become a typical example of his entire production.

♦ JOHN FIELD
Pianist and composer, born in Dublin (1782–1837) (left, in a portrait), Field was a student of Muzio Clementi. He is the father of piano nocturnes.

CHOPIN PLAYS FOR HIS FRIENDS
Compared to Liszt or his other fellow pianists, Chopin gave very few concerts. He did not like audiences or big concert halls, considering them unsuitable to his way of playing very delicate pieces. In his home, however, he often performed for a few friends until late in the night.

♦ AUGUSTE FRANCHOMME
A violoncellist at the *Théâtre des Italiens* and at the Conservatory, Chopin dedicated to him his *Sonata in G Minor for Cello and Piano*, op. 65.

♦ FRANZ LISZT
A piano virtuoso known all over Europe, he became a good friend of Chopin, who dedicated his *12 Études*, op. 10 to him.

♦ MARIE D'AGOULT
In 1835, at thirty, she left her husband to follow Liszt, with whom she would have three children. Chopin dedicated his *12 Études,* op. 25 to her.

♦ **POLISH FRIENDS**
In Paris, Chopin befriended Wojciech Grzymala and again found his boyhood companions, Julian Fontana, who emigrated to America in 1841, and Jan Matuszynski, who died of tuberculosis in 1842.

♦ **THE SYMBOL OF THE NIGHT**
As a symbol of mystery, darkness, solitude, dreams, nightmares, and passion, the night is clearly the part of the day that the romantics preferred. *Hymn to Night* (1799) by Novalis (above, in a portrait) began a period of poems, novels, dramas, and nocturnal landscapes illuminated more or less by poetic "moonlight." Even in music, there are compositions inspired by the night. Besides the many theatrical operas and *Lieder* set in the night, there is Mendelssohn's *Nocturne* in the stage music for *Midsummer Night's Dream* and the cantata based upon Goethe's text, the "First Walpurgis Night." Among the piano works, there are the *21 Nocturnes* by Chopin, the *4 Nachtstücke*, op. 23, and "The Sabbath Night's Dream," the fifth piece of the *Fantastic*, op. 12 of Robert Schumann, and *In Dreams*, a nocturne by Liszt.

8. CHOPIN'S LIFE ♦ *Chopin had few problems in 1840, even though he again began to cough up blood during the winter. On April 26, 1841 Chopin played at the Salle Pleyel. For his first semipublic concert after six years, he chose his favorite formula: No more than three hundred people in the hall and tickets were to cost twenty francs. The evening was a success, underlined in the* Gazette Musicale *by Liszt's enthusiastic review. In December he performed for King Louis-Philippe for the last time. Later, his friend Julian Fontana, who helped him as a copyist and secretary, immigrated to America.* ⇒

THE ORCHESTRA DIRECTOR

Until the time of Beethoven, the figure of the orchestra director was poorly defined. It was the composer himself or the first violinist who led the orchestra. During the time of romanticism, scores became more elaborate, orchestral ensembles increased, and the paying audiences of concert societies required the presence of a specialized musician. He supervised everything from orchestra rehearsals to directing the concert. Linked to this phenomenon and the increasing practice—even during piano performances—of playing other musicians' pieces was the birth of the modern concept of musical interpretation. The romantic aesthetics strongly supported the appearance of this dominant figure who was capable of understanding the composer's intentions and conveying them to the public.

♦ THE PIONEERS
OF MODERN
ORCHESTRATION
The first great romantic composer to have contributed to the birth of modern orchestration is Weber. Although in a lithography of 1826 he is portrayed directing with a roll of music (above), he often used a baton and score while standing up. He was distinguished for the precision of his rehearsals and for the care he put into the layout of the orchestra. Mendelssohn followed his example; moreover, he transformed the orchestra in Leipzig Gewandhaus into one of the best in the world. He performed music by Mozart, Beethoven, and other contemporaries, and contributed to the concept of musical repertory by directing long-forgotten compositions, such as Bach's *Passion according to St. Matthew*, at that time not heard for one hundred years, and several oratorios by Händel.

LEIPZIG, 1839:
THE REDISCOVERY OF SCHUBERT
For the first time, Mendelssohn directed Schubert's *Symphony in C Major*, discovered in Vienna by Schumann. It is a monumental work, considered for a long time to be too difficult. Even in 1842 and 1844, the orchestras of London and Paris rejected it.

♦ THE USE OF
THE SCORE
It spread very slowly. Even a remarkable director like Habeneck played first violin by using only a few handwritten notes.

♦ THEORIES OF CONDUCTING
The golden rules of the modern director are summed up in Berlioz' *Le chef d'orchestre: théorie de son art*, published in 1844 as an appendix to his *Treatise on Instrumentation* and in Richard Wagner's essay of 1869 entitled *The Art of Conducting*. Wagner is another important figure in the history of orchestra conducting.

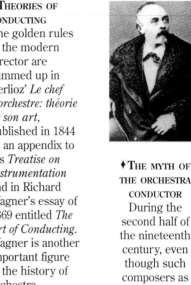

♦ THE MYTH OF THE ORCHESTRA CONDUCTOR
During the second half of the nineteenth century, even though such composers as Brahms, Bruckner, Dvorák, and Tchaikovsky continued to publicly interpret their own works, the professional figure of the orchestra conductor appeared. He was a musician who was also a composer, but who specialized as well in directing the music of others. At the same time, and according to the concept of a musical repertoire, in many European cities and even in America, full orchestras were established. Many of them are still active today, such as the Philharmonics of Vienna, New York, and Berlin. The German Hans von Bülow (above) and Hans Richter, student and son-in-law of Liszt, were among the founders of the modern concept of orchestra direction.

♦ THE BATON
Many conductors continued to direct with a violin bow or a rolled-up sheet of music. Thanks to Weber, Spohr, Mendelssohn, and Berlioz, however, the baton became fashionable.

♦ THE CONDUCTOR RAISES UP
Berlioz believed that the larger the orchestra, the higher the podium should be in order to allow everyone to see the conductor.

THE LAYOUT OF THE ORCHESTRA
In some orchestras, such as that of Meiningen, directed by von Bülow from 1880 to 1885, musicians still performed standing up.

BEYOND THE SONATA

Except for Berlioz, the greatest romantic composers were all extraordinary pianists who wrote extensively for their instrument. Compared to the composers of the preceding generation, however, they rarely composed great pieces such as the sonata, which is built on several movements and is based on the idea of development. They chose to write smaller pieces that were simpler in form in order to decisively express their own feelings. This is the case of the *Songs without Words* by Mendelssohn, and the nocturnes, the impromptus, or mazurkas by Chopin. They also preferred broader compositions, but ones having freer and more formal structures than the sonata. These are formed by a succession of short pieces—as in Schumann's case—and express the inner conflicts of their own universe. Chopin's *Ballades* are a relevant exception.

◆ **THE DECLINE OF THE SONATA**
In 1822 Beethoven stopped writing piano sonatas, after having written thirty-two. Five years later, the eighteen-year-old Mendelssohn also abandoned the sonata. Schumann was twenty-six years old when he finished the last of his three sonatas. Chopin's case was slightly different. He composed a sonata when he was eighteen years old and returned to it with two important and original works in 1839 and 1844. Both Schumann and Chopin coped poorly with traditional formal rules, and Liszt did not follow them at all. He made his only sonata (above, a page of the score, written between 1852 and 1853) into a single thirty-minute movement, combining the contrasts of the first movement and the contrasts between movements, typical of the classical sonata.

POLISH FOLK DANCES
Chopin listened to the peasants' music and the folk songs of his boyhood village during his summer vacation in Szafarnia and Kowalewo, in Kujawia.

◆ **THE POEMS OF ADAM MICKIEWICZ**
Schumann felt that Chopin's *Ballades* were the musical version of some poems by Mickiewicz (1798–1855). They have some elements in common, but mostly relating only to atmosphere. Above, Warsaw's old market square.

The great elasticity of Polish folk rhythmic values is the basis of Chopin's famous *rubato* (a change in speed against a steady accompaniment).

♦ **THE BALLADES**
Chopin (above) seldom used classical forms rich in history and tradition for his major works. Instead, he used atypical forms such as the scherzo and the polonaise, which he completely reworked, and new forms such as the ballade. The latter seems to summarize in an original way some of the formal characteristics of the first movement of a sonata, a rondo, and a variation. Composed between 1831 and 1842, his four *Ballades* have nothing to do with the dance. They evoke a poetic form that is typical of romantic poetry, often set to music, with which it shares the narrative, epic, and lyrical tone.

♦ **THE MAZURKA**
A lively dance of Mazowia, the mazurka is characterized by triple time and the accentuation of weak beats. Chopin wrote 52 mazurkas.

THE POLONAISE
This is a moderate dance in three-quarter time. Chopin composed 19 polonaises, of which his last works are extremely intense and dramatic.

THE CONSERVATORIES

After the era of Haydn, Mozart, and Beethoven, and on the wave of the splendid romanticism, German music rose to become a role model in the instrumental and symphonic fields. German conservatories became a hallmark for the study of composition and musical theory. In Italy, where the tradition and the term *conservatory* were born, music schools trained only singers and operatic artists. The situation was slightly better in France. At the Paris Conservatory, composition classes were led by the most fashionable opera stars, and even the excellent piano classes were not open to non-French citizens, as the Hungarian Liszt discovered to his great disappointment. In Russia the first conservatory opened in 1862 in Saint Petersburg.

♦ **THE SUCCESS OF LEIPZIG**
After a failed attempt in Berlin, with the support of King Friedrich Wilhelm IV, Mendelssohn established a conservatory in Leipzig (above, a view of the town). Opened in 1843, it had a remarkable staff: Mendelssohn taught piano, ensemble music and later composition, Schumann taught piano and composition, Ferdinand David taught violin, Moritz Hauptmann taught harmony and counterpoint, Carl Ferdinand Becker taught organ, theory, and music history, Henriette Grabau-Bünau and Ferdinand Böhme taught choral and solo singing and, beginning in 1846, Moscheles taught the advanced piano classes. The twenty-two students at the beginning doubled in three months. There were sixty by the end of the year, and two hundred and five in 1847. Twenty-seven years after its founding, fifteen hundred students had studied there.

A MODEL SCHOOL
Mendelssohn demanded that all the students attend chamber music classes, pass secondary or core examinations, and organize student concerts.

♦ **FERDINAND DAVID**
Born in 1810, he was the first violin of the *Gewandhaus* and the first to interpret Mendelssohn's *Concerto for Violin*.

♦ **SEPARATE CLASSES**
There were no mixed classes in the German conservatory. Male students were strictly separated from their female counterparts.

♦ **THE LEIPZIG CONSERVATORY** The building that hosts the Leipzig Conservatory was a two-story palace built by the town council in the Gewandhaus court.

♦ **AN INTERNATIONAL SCHOOL** Convinced of the superiority of German music, Mendelssohn opened his Conservatory to foreign students. The first year, they numbered seven out of sixty, or 11 percent of the entire student population. This percentage increased steadily until it reached 54 percent in 1869, when fifty-six out of one hundred and three enrolled students were not German. Between 1843 and 1869, out of a total of fifteen hundred students, one-third were foreigners from other European countries overseas. A high number of students (126) were from England, where Mendelssohn and Moscheles were very popular. Russia was represented by eighty-five students, the Scandinavian countries with forty-eight, including the Norwegian, Edvard Grieg (above). The United States was represented by one hundred students between 1851 and 1869.

♦ **JOSEPH JOACHIM** Born in 1831, he was one of the most important violinists of the nineteenth century. He dedicated his *Concerto* to Brahms, and in 1868 he began to direct the Berlin Conservatory.

PRIVATE LESSONS

Private piano lessons were flourishing. All the greatest instrumentalists, such as Kalkbrenner, Moscheles, and Herz, were in great demand as teachers. A few months after his arrival in Paris, Chopin became the most fashionable private teacher in the capital. He gave up to eight or nine lessons per day, and among his students were many young women of the aristocracy and upper middle class, such as Princess Marcellina Czartoriska and Baroness Charlotte de Rotschild. The increase in private lessons also favored the increase in the great number of methods by which one could study the piano, and also of some bizarre but effective devices that were aimed at helping the student maintain a correct posture during the long hours of training.

A SUCCESSFUL TEACHER
For a private lesson, Chopin received twenty francs (later twenty-five). Kalkbrenner, who had the highest fees in Europe, received more or less the same amount.

♦ THE EDUCATIONAL REPERTORY
In his teaching, Chopin used the *Études* by Clementi, Cramer, and Moscheles, and the *Well-Tempered Clavier* by Bach.

♦ TWO PIANOS FOR ONE LESSON
During his lessons, Chopin sometimes played more than his students, using an upright Pleyel piano.

♦ GEORGES
MATHIAS
A professor
at the Paris
Conservatory, he
was considered
the recipient
of Chopin's
piano secrets.

♦ CARL CZERNY: A VALUABLE MENTOR
A student of Beethoven in Vienna
and Liszt's teacher, Czerny (1791–1857)
is remembered more as an educator
and an author of hundreds of
studies and exercises of great
value than as a composer.

♦ METHODS AND
DEVICES
Besides a
comprehensive
educational group
of progressive
exercises and
studies, many
pianists wrote
techniques for
the study of
piano. Here, they
summarized their
ideas in terms of
hand position,
how to organize
their study,
instrumental
technique, and
the style of
execution. After
the contributions
by Dussek,
Clementi, and
Adam, works by
Cramer (1815),
Hummel (1828),
Kalkbrenner
(1830), Fétis, and
Moscheles (1837,
with the bold title
of *Method of
Methods*), and
Czerny (1839)
appeared. Even
Chopin wrote
one, but left it
unfinished. As to
educational
tools (above,
an example),
the case of
Schumann is
tragic. In 1832,
while using a
device to
reinforce his
ring finger—the
weakest by
nature—he
severely injured
himself, forever
ending his
concert career.

♦ CARL FILTSCH
He did not
become a second
Liszt as he had
hoped. The young
Hungarian died in
1845 at the age of
fifteen, at the peak
of his career.

9. CHOPIN'S LIFE ♦ *On February 21, 1842, Chopin
played again at the Salle Pleyel, repeating his great
success of the year before. On that same day, in Warsaw,
his first teacher, Wojciech Zywny, died. On April 20 his
best friend, Jan Matuszynski, a guest of his in Paris, died
of tuberculosis. During the first months of 1843 his
health worsened; and after a peaceful summer spent at
Nohant that year, at the beginning of 1844, things again
got worse and at the end of May Chopin was saddened by
the death of his father, Nicolas. In July his sister Ludwika
came to see him after fourteen years.* ⇒▸

THE MYTH OF BEETHOVEN

One of the many contradictions of romanticism is its relationship with Beethoven. Beethoven appears as the precursor of the "romantic school of music." In 1836 Schumann wrote that the progressive composers of his time were "Beethovenian." He placed them "on the left wing" alongside an ideal political alignment for being "young, bold followers of geniality, and carefree form." Beethoven's constant attachment to precise formal models distanced him from the romantics. In addition, the value of his production inhibited his romantic production, especially regarding the symphony and the piano sonata.

EUROPEANS HONOR BEETHOVEN
Bonn, August 12, 1845:
A monument commemorates the 75th anniversary of Beethoven's birth. Liszt had collected most of the funds.

♦**THREE DAYS OF CELEBRATIONS**
On August 11, the first day of celebrations, Ludwig Spohr (above) conducted Beethoven's *Missa Solemnis* and the *Ninth Symphony*, then all the guests boarded the boat *Ludwig van Beethoven* for Nonnenwerth Island, where a banquet awaited them. The following morning, Liszt conducted the *Missa in C Major* inside Bonn's cathedral. Later, after visiting the monument, Liszt conducted the *Fifth Symphony* and the finale of *Fidelio*. He played the *Fifth Concerto* under the direction of Spohr in the Festhalle, the three-thousand-seat hall he had commissioned. On August 13 Liszt conducted the *Cantata for the Inauguration of Beethoven's Monument* in Bonn, his first symphonic-choral composition. The huge outdoor banquet was ruined by a violent storm, which ended the celebrations.

♦**THE PUBLIC**
Among those present were the pianist Camille Moke-Pleyel, the dancer Lola Montez, and Anton Schindler, Beethoven's secretary.

♦**QUEENS AND KINGS**
Many crowned heads attended the ceremony to honor Beethoven. Among them were the king of Prussia, Friedrich Wilhelm IV and his wife, and Queen Victoria and Prince Albert of England. Among the musicians were Berlioz, Meyerbeer, and Moscheles.

♦ **An album for Beethoven**
In 1841 the Viennese publisher Mechetti published an album that contained ten pieces by various composers, among them Chopin's *Prélude in C Sharp Minor*, op. 45 and Mendelssohn's *Variations sérieuses*. The profits helped pay for the building of the monument to Beethoven (left, in an 1844 portrait).

♦ **The statue**
The work of the sculptor Ernst-Julius Hähnel cost 50,000 francs. Liszt contributed 10,000 francs.

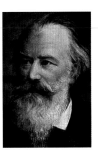

♦ **The "Tenth"**
The post-Beethoven uneasiness toward the symphony was clear in the case of Johannes Brahms (above). Rejecting the modern tendency for program music and the symphonic poem, he began his *First Symphony* in 1862. He did not finish it until 1876, when he was forty-three and had already composed a series of piano masterpieces, chamber music, and other orchestral works. Twenty-five years had passed since the last symphony by Schumann, and in Germany, the proud home of the symphony, there was great suspense. Eduard Hanslick, the most important Viennese critic of his time, compared the *First* to the great symphonies by Beethoven, while Hans von Bülow called it the "Tenth of Beethoven." In so doing, he showed not only an anachronistic mockery, but also his wish to continue in the strict formal tradition.

THE DISCOVERY OF THE TIMBRE

A great novelty of romantic music is the attention to sounds, that is, to the expressive resources of the voices of single instruments—the timbre—and their possible combinations. In symphonic music, the orchestral palette is enriched by using such traditional instruments as the clarinet and the horn in new ways, and by introducing to opera instruments such as the harp and the English horn. Also, the percussion and wind sections expanded with a proportional increase of bows. In piano music, the great evolution of the instruments allowed for a more refined use of timbre shades and sound volumes.

ROMEO AND JULIET
In this "dramatic symphony," composed in 1839 and dedicated to Paganini, Berlioz made the process of orchestra evolution more mature. This had already been attempted with his *Fantastic Symphony* and *Harold in Italy*.

♦ **THE COLORS OF THE ORCHESTRA**
In *Romeo and Juliet*, Berlioz doubled the use of the harp and the triangle for their particular timbre, along with the timpani.

♦ **THE SCORE**
After hearing *Romeo and Juliet*, Théophile Gautier wrote: "Berlioz has given a soul to every instrument."

♦ **HUMAN INSTRUMENTS**
The oboe is used predominantly to represent Juliet. The bows and, especially, the cello, represent Romeo.

♦ **CYMBALS AND DRUMS**
In addition to the bass drum and the Basque drums, Berlioz required the use of cymbals of various dimensions in the score of *Romeo and Juliet*.

Chopin impressed his contemporaries with his way of playing the piano. The critic, Fétis, found that Chopin's ability to endlessly vary the different shades of strength, sweetness, and accent was "marvelous." In Chopin's obituary in the *Gazette Musicale*, it was written, "Another bit and it would have vanished into the intangible and imperceptible." This great sensitivity to sound exists of course even with Chopin as a composer, and in particular in his late compositions. The *Berceuse in D Flat*, op. 57, the *Barcarolle in F Sharp*, op. 60, the *Polonaise-Fantasie in A Flat*, op. 61 (above, the frontispiece, and the *Nocturnes*, op. 62, composed in 1843–1846) show that the fine line between melody and harmony was fading. It was giving way to a new sound, often made of "spots" of color, leading to impressionism.

10. CHOPIN'S LIFE ♦ *Chopin spent his summers in Nohant, but his relationship with George Sand began to fall apart. In November 1846 he returned to Paris to give private lessons, especially to his Scottish student, Jane Stirling. He was also a witness at the wedding of his friend Bodhan Zaleski, for whom he set some poems to music. George Sand decided to stay in Nohant all winter. In July 1847, at the end of a period full of tension and misunderstandings, the two separated. Chopin's health grew worse.* ⟫→

THE SYMPHONIC POEM

Around the middle of the century, Liszt created a genre of orchestral music that had great success: the symphonic poem. A few past examples of program music such as the overtures of Beethoven and Mendelssohn written for the theatrical drama, and Berlioz' works (*Fantastic Symphony* and *Harold in Italy*) influenced him. The symphonic poem is different from the symphony in that, generally, it has one movement instead of four, and it is inspired by nonmusical ideas—literary, pictorial, naturalistic, or historic. Since then, the symphony, with a few important exceptions such as Beethoven's *Pastoral*, has always represented the supreme achievement of "absolute music."

♦ **THE CYCLIC FORM**
Usually, symphonic poems are single-movement compositions with alternating sections in different tempo and one or more returning themes heard at the beginning. Ideally, this genre concentrates the contrasting characteristics of the different movements of a symphony or a sonata and those of the three parts forming the first tempo of a sonata-like composition— exposition, development, and recapitulation. This type of structure, called a "cyclic form," is not exclusive to the symphonic poem. Other important romantic compositions, such as the *Sonata in B Minor for Piano* by Liszt feature it. Even Schumann's *Fourth Symphony* is based on a theme that recurs in four movements, initially conceived by the composer without continuity (above, a page of the score).

♦ **ARTISTS AND HEROES**
Liszt saw the fall and rise of the hero as the metaphor for the existence of genius.

♦ **LORD GEORGE BYRON,**
A ROMANTIC HERO
Born in London in 1788, handsome and aristocratic, with an adventurous life, Lord Byron personified the heroes of his fantasies. He died at thirty-six in Greece, where he was organizing a national revolt.

♦ **A PROLIFIC MUSICIAN**
Between 1848 and 1882 Liszt composed thirteen symphonic poems, inspired by, among others, Shakespeare, Hugo, and Goethe.

1851: Liszt composes "Mazeppa"
Ivan Mazeppa, a seventeenth-century Polish aristocrat, was condemned for having seduced a count's wife. He was tied behind a horse that was sent galloping through the plains of the Ukraine. Rescued by the Cossacks, he became their chief.

♦ **Mazeppa's wild ride**
Taken from works by Byron and Hugo, the story also inspired a piano étude by Liszt, written before the symphonic poem.

♦ **The post-Liszt period**
In the second half of the nineteenth century, the symphonic poem became, along with opera, one of the favorite genres of the composers from the "national schools." Its enhanced musical flavor encouraged this leaning. These composers wrote a series of scores inspired by national literary works or the legends of various countries. The case of *My Country*, the cycle of seven symphonic poems, composed between 1874 and 1879 by the Czech, Bedřich Smetana, is an example. Its most famous piece, "The Moldau," describes the course of the river that runs through Prague. However, the absolute masterpieces of this kind of music were born with the works of the German Richard Strauss (1864–1949) (above, in a portrait), composer of such pieces as *Don Juan* (1889), a work of unsurpassed virtuosity.

CHOPIN'S LEGACY

Chopin left no heirs as a pianist, because, in spite of his many students, he did not start a school, and, as a composer, he had only imitators and followers. Due to the content of his production and relevant autobiographical events such as fleeing from his oppressed country, his tuberculosis, and his early death, he is viewed today as the ultimate romantic composer. In the second half of the nineteenth century, this image became even more magnified. A procession of young ladies were enraptured by his *Nocturnes* and concert pianists performed his music with emotion. Critics and artists provided a different interpretation of his music during our century, thus acknowledging the influence his late masterpieces have had on twentieth-century music.

♦ CRITICS
Chopin (above in an 1849 daguerreotype) has been criticized essentially for three reasons: the morbid nature of his music, his inability to deal with great forms, and the absence of orchestral compositions. The first has no basis; his contemporaries, unable to understand his music, mixed the elements of life and art together. The second, championed by the Frenchman Vincent d'Indy, blended him with the other romantics, regarding his original formal choices as deviations from the lessons of the Viennese School. As for the third— perhaps the last to die—the opposite is true. Chopin used the orchestra up until his twenties and then added to his work a mixture of small but pleasant tone color inventions.

A SOLEMN FUNERAL
October 30, 1849, at the Church of La Madeleine, Paris. All the important Parisians, except George Sand, attended Chopin's funeral. During the ceremony, the *Requiem* by Mozart was played.

♦ LUIGI LABLACHE
Born in Naples, Lablache was the greatest bass singer of the time. He sang at Beethoven's funeral and was Thalberg's father-in-law.

♦ THE FUNERAL PROCESSION
Meyerbeer, Prince Czartoryski, Delacroix, Gutmann, and Franchomme were among those attending the funeral.

THE GRAVE
Chopin is buried in the Père Lachaise Cemetery, but his heart is buried in a pillar of the Church of the Holy Cross in Warsaw, Poland.

♦ **JANE STIRLING**
A loyal student, this rich woman from Scotland helped Chopin financially in his last months, even paying the expenses for his funeral.

♦ **A HUGE CROWD**
More than three thousand invited guests gathered in the church, while many other people remained outside.

♦ **PLAYING CHOPIN**
Along with that of Liszt, Chopin's music has always been present in the repertoire of every pianist. To talk about the great interpreters of Chopin is to talk about the history of piano playing. Three interpreters whom the public invariably associate with him are the Pole, Jan Ignacy Paderewski (1886–1982), the Frenchman, Alfred Cortot (1877–1962), and another Pole, Artur Rubinstein (1886–1982). The Russian, Sergei Rachmaninov (1873–1943) (above) was among the first to take any sentimentalism from the music of Chopin and emphasize instead its most noble and tragic elements. Since 1927, there has been a competition in Warsaw dedicated to Chopin, rewarding some of today's most talented performers of his music such as Maurizio Pollini (1942–), Martha Argerich (1941–), and Krystian Zimerman (1956–).

♦ **PAULINE VIARDOT-GARCIA**
A very famous singer, student, and friend of Chopin, she sang Mozart's *Requiem* with Lablache.

11. CHOPIN'S LIFE ♦ *On February 16, 1848, Chopin played at the Salle Pleyel. Almost six hundred people could not get a ticket. It became impossible to give lessons during the Revolution and this reduced his income. In April he traveled to England, where in seven months he gave nine concerts, as many as he had given in Paris in ten years. In November he returned to Paris in very poor health. In April 1849 he "dragged himself" (as Delacroix wrote) to the première of Meyerbeer's* The Prophet. *In August his sister Ludwika visited him, and the following month he moved to the apartment in the Place Vendôme, where he died on October 17.* ➠

ROMANTIC MUSIC

Undoubtedly, romanticism can be considered the era of the piano. Today, hundreds of thousands of pianos of all sizes take their place of honor in all Western homes. In concert halls, a generation of virtuosos of the keyboard play with wizardry. Thanks to Liszt, Moscheles, Mendelssohn, and Chopin, the way of conceiving a piano concerto has changed radically. The idea of a musical repertoire in the hands of a single piano interpreter was born. The idea of this new figure perfectly embodied the romantic vision of an inspired artist who was able to re-create a work of art while executing it. The piano became the instrument that best expressed the smallest emotions, when played like Chopin or a poet of sounds like Schumann.

Thanks to ever more refined instruments, the conception of the new romantic sound developed. Even the orchestra, especially because of Weber and Berlioz, changed its voice, and the romantics looked for original forms for the symphony, eventually creating the symphonic poem. However, romanticism is the era of contradictions and, in the musical production of the great composers, striking oddities can be found. Mendelssohn and Schumann, closer to the German tradition, tested themselves in almost any musical genre, but Chopin wrote only for piano, completely ignoring symphony and opera music, and Berlioz, a genius with the orchestra, did not play the piano at all.

MUSIC FOR PIANO

During his career, Chopin composed only for piano, making him an exception in the history of music. Long criticized by some as incapable of writing for the great musical forms, Chopin actually created works that blend extraordinary vigor and poetic sensibility. They are the four *Ballades* (op. 23, op. 38, op. 47, and op. 52), the four *Scherzi* (op. 20, op. 31, op. 39, and op. 54), and the 1841 *Fantasy in F Minor*, op. 49. The *24 Preludes*, op. 28 are indeed sketches that sometimes last only a few seconds, but they are constructed according to a superb architectural sense in all the twenty-four tonalities of the tempered scale. The same internal coherence, apart from its divine artistic and technical qualities, sustains the two series of *Études* op. 10 and op. 25. The seventeen *Polonaises* came from the music of his native country. They have heroic and passionate tones, such as the famous *Polonaise in A Flat Major,* op. 53 of 1842, and creations that are innovative at formal and tone levels such as the *Polonaise-Fantasy in A Flat Major,* op. 61 of 1846. The more than fifty *Mazurkas* occupy a very special place in Chopin's production. In a way, they represent an intimate diary; however, they do not enjoy the popularity of his other more delightful compositions such as the *Waltz,* the four *Impromptus* or the twenty-one *Nocturnes.* His late works are particularly fascinating for their tone refinement. Among them, the following isolated pieces shine on their own: the *Prelude in C Sharp Minor,* op. 45, the *Berceuse in D Flat Major* op. 57, and the *Barcarolle in F Sharp Major,* op. 60. As for the sonatas, after the *Sonata in C Minor,* op. 4, composed at eighteen, Chopin finished only two others, but they were very important works. They are the *Sonata no. 2 in B Flat Minor,* op. 35 of 1839, constructed around an incredible funeral march where Schumann saw "something repulsive," and the *Sonata no. 3 in B Minor,* op. 58 of 1844.

Schumann, the other exquisite poet of the piano, followed a different path. Most of his piano masterpieces were produced between 1829 and 1839. They were devoted entirely to the piano and were full of thematic echoes and continual references to the real and literary world of the composer. The case of the *Davidsbündlertänze,* op. 6 (*Dances of the David-leaguers*), which was not signed but had the subtitle of "character pieces composed by Florestan and Eusebius," is an example. Schumann's favorite form was the cycle of "character pieces"—*Davidsbündlertänze,* op. 6, the *Phantasiestücke,* op. 12 (*Fantasy piece*), *Kinderszenenen,* op. 15 (*Scenes from Childhood*), or the polyptych formed by several panels such as *Butterflies,* op. 2, *Carnaval,* op. 9, and *Kreisleriana,* op. 16. With the *Sonata no. 1 in F Sharp Minor,* op. 11, the *Concert sans Orchestre in F Minor,* op. 14, (revised later as *Sonata no. 3*), the *Fantasy in C Major,* op. 17, and the *Sonata no. 2 in G Minor,* op. 22, he tried other forms. The *Concert Studies on Paganini Caprices,* op. 3 and op. 10 and the *Symphonic Studies,* op. 13 are remarkable works. Among the works written after 1840, the forty-three pieces of the *Album für die Jugend,* op. 68, the nine *Waldscenen,* op. 82, 1848–1849, and the beautiful five *Morning Songs,* op. 133, ended his piano production of 1853.

By looking only at the 1850s, Liszt's piano production appears endless and of unequal quality. The various collections of *Études,* the first two collections of *Années de Pélerinage* (*Years of Pilgrimmage*), a sort of romantic musical diary that evokes nature and works of art that inspired him during his journeys, and the *Sonata in B minor* (1852–1853), a unique contribution of its kind, are milestones of his career. *Poetic and Religious Harmonies,* (1845–1852), where the two main aspects of his personality blend and the first fifteen *Hungarian Rhapsodies* (1851–1853), a stylized evocation of Gypsy music, are worth remembering. A side chapter of his production, important from the artistic point of view is that of the arrangements and transcriptions. In addition to an infinite number of successful paraphrases and fantasies from lyrical operas, the arrangements for solo piano of *Lieder* by Schubert and Schumann, the transcription of music for organ by Bach, and those of great symphonic works such as the nine sym-

phonies by Beethoven, and the *Fantastic* by Berlioz are noteworthy.

Mendelssohn is known for having created the genre of *Lied ohne Worte* (*Song without Words*), of which forty-eight piano pieces appear divided into eight groups, one of the most refined expressions of salon music. His other works worth remembering are the brilliant *Rondo Capriccioso,* op. 14 of 1830, the *Fantasy in F Sharp Minor,* op. 28, called the "Scottish Sonata" of 1833 and the *Variations Sérieuses in D Minor,* op. 54 of 1841.

Even if Weber's production is undervalued today, it still plays an important role in the evolution of the romantic piano sound, especially in pieces such as the *Sonata no. 2 in A Flat Major,* op. 39 (1816), *Invitation to the Dance* (1819), op. 65, and the *Sonata no. 4 in E Minor,* op. 70 (1822).

CHAMBER MUSIC

Weber left no relevant works in the field of chamber music; Berlioz and Liszt ignored it completely. There are four works by Chopin (all with piano), two created in Warsaw and two written in Paris for his friend Franchomme, among which the *Sonata in G Minor for Piano and Violoncello,* op. 65 of 1846 stands out.

After the magnificent *Octet in E Flat Major for Strings,* op. 20, written at sixteen, Mendelssohn wrote a dozen works among which the *String Quartets nos. 3–5,* op. 44 (1837–1838) and the *Piano Trio in D Minor,* op. 49 (1839) emerge.

Schumann's production is not vast, but it contains several important pieces such as the *Three String Quartets,* op. 41 of 1842, the *Three Trios for Piano and Strings* op. 63 and op. 80 of 1847, and op. 110 of 1851, the *Two Sonatas for Violin and Piano* of 1851, and at least two masterpieces, the *Quintet in E Flat Major for Piano and Strings,* op. 44 and the *Quartet in E Flat Major for Piano and Strings,* op. 47, both written in 1842.

LIEDER AND VOCAL MELODIES

Cultivated by Weber, Mendelssohn, and Schubert, the *Lied* was mastered by Schumann. Most of his *Lieder* were written in 1840, the year of his marriage to Clara, and is dedicated to love. Among the more than one hundred and twenty *Lieder* written that year and distributed in twenty cycles, there are the nine *Lieder,* op. 24, to a text by Heine, the twelve *Lieder,* op. 39, to texts by Eichendorff, and the two cycles that may mark the climax of the romantic *Lied, Frauenliebe und leben,* op. 42 (*Woman's Love and Life*) to texts by Chamisso and *Dicterliebe,* op. 48 (*Poet's Love*) to texts by Heine.

Liszt composed about fifty German Lieder, mostly during the second half of the century—in addition to others based on French, Italian, Hungarian, and English texts—all unfairly undervalued. Chopin's seventeen Polish songs, op. 74, composed between 1827 and 1847, and published posthumously in 1855, are also rarely heard. Even Berlioz composed several melodies, including *Summer Nights,* op. 7, a series of six lyrics to a text by Théophile Gautier, composed in 1840–1841, which stand out.

SYMPHONIES

In spite of the strong stimulus given by Weber to the romantic orchestra, his two *Symphonies* of 1807 are unimportant works. Mendelssohn wrote five *Symphonies* for the grand orchestra. Schumann wrote only four; however, there exists a discrepancy between their numbering order, linked to their publication, and that of their composition. After the *Symphony no. 1 in C Minor,* op. 11 of 1824, the second *Symphony* finished by Mendelssohn is called *Symphony no. 5 in D Minor,* op. 107, known as "Reformation," composed in 1830 for the third centennial of the Augsburg Confession. Mendelssohn disliked it and it was not published until 1868. Of his own *Symphonies* conceived in 1829–1831, the one in A major, the "Italian" of 1833, owes its title of *Symphony no. 4,* op. 90 to its publication in 1851, while that in A minor, known as the "Scottish" was published in 1842 as *Symphony no, 3,* op. 56. Among them is the *Symphony no. 2 in B Flat Major,* op. 52 "*Song of Praise*" of 1840, conceived as a cantata with solo voices and chorus.

As for Schumann, in 1841 he finished his *Symphony no. 1 in B Flat Major,* op. 38 and a second *Symphony in D Minor* that was discarded after its first performance. Those that we have today are the *Symphony no. 2 in C Major,* op. 61 of 1846, and *Symphony no. 3 in E Flat Major,* op. 97, called "*Rhenish,*" of 1850. They are in reality the third and fourth. The *Symphony no. 4 in D Minor,* op. 120, of 1851 was the updated version of the symphony discarded in 1841.

Outside Germany, the most innovative contribution to the symphony was that of Berlioz with his *Fantastic Symphony,* op. 14 of 1830, based on an almost theatrical program. His next attempts distanced him even more from the traditional form. *Harold in Italy,* op. 16, "with solo viola" of 1834, inspired by Byron, is halfway between a symphony, a symphonic poem, and a sinfonia concertante (symphony with one or more solo instruments), *Romeo and Juliet,* op. 17, a "dramatic symphony" for solo chorus and orchestra of 1839 leads to the opera.

Even Liszt's two symphonies, the *Faust Symphony* and the *Dante Symphony* (1854–1856), are based on a program and contain voices and chorus.

CONCERTS

Chopin used the orchestra only in his piano and orchestra music from 1827 to 1830. Before leaving Warsaw, the young pianist-composer felt the need to create a repertoire. The *Concerto in F Minor,* composed in 1829–1830 and published in 1836 as *no. 2,* op. 21, and the *Concerto in E Minor,* published as *no. 1,* op. 11 in 1833, although written as the second in 1830, are preceded by the *Variations on Là ci darem la mano,* op. 2, by Mozart, by the *Grande Fantaisie on Polish Airs,* op. 13, and by the *Krakowiak,* op. 14. After the *Grande Polonaise Brillante,* op. 22 of 1830, Chopin abandoned the use of the orchestra.

Weber contributed to this genre not so much with his two *Concertos* (1810–1812) in the Biedermeier style, but with some elements of his *Konzertstück in F Minor,* op. 79 of 1821. These elements are: the use of virtuosity for dramatic purposes, the structure in a single tempo articulated in sections of diverse modulations, and the reference to a program—the story of a crusader who returns from the Holy Land—even though this last one was eventually abandoned by Weber himself.

Mendelssohn's works are exquisitely constructed, even though they are less important. They are the *Concerto no. 1 in G Minor,* op. 25 of 1831 and the *Concerto no. 2 in D minor,* op. 40 of 1837. They are compensated by the marvelous *Concerto in E Minor for Violin and Orchestra,* op. 64, a masterpiece in the genre of romantic concert music. It was performed for the first time by David in 1845. Its piano equivalent is the *Concerto in A Minor,* op. 54 by Schumann, a great work for its high poetic contents and the splendid blend between the pianist and the orchestra. Not so well thought of are the other two excellent *Concertos* by Schumann: the *Concerto in A Minor for Violoncello,* op. 129, composed in 1850, but performed posthumously four years later, and the *Concerto in D Minor for Violin,* composed by Joachim in 1853, and performed for the first time in 1937.

Liszt's piano and orchestra compositions all appeared during the second half of the century. The final version of the *Concerto no. 1 in E Flat Major* was begun in 1830 and produced in 1855. The first draft of the *Concerto no. 2 in A Major,* published in 1863, was written in 1839. In both these concertos, Liszt experimented with the cyclic form and skillfully blended piano and orchestra. The *Totentanz* (*Dance of the Dead*), a diabolic paraphrase of the Gregorian theme of the *Dies Irae,* conceived in 1838, and performed for the first time in 1865, is worth remembering.

OVERTURES AND SYMPHONIC POEMS

In addition to the masterpiece written for *Midsummer Night's Dream,* Mendelssohn composed other overtures, among which are *Calm Sea and Prosperous Voyage,* op. 27 of 1828, inspired by two poems by Goethe, and *The Hebrides,* op. 26, of 1830–1833, composed after a visit to the Nordic islands. They all evoke the symphonic poem for their vivid recollection of nature. Berlioz' *overtures* follow the same line. Among them are "The Roman Carnival," op. 9, and "The Privateer," op. 21 of 1844, and the three composed by Schumann in 1850–1851. Liszt is the father of the symphonic poem. Between 1848 and 1858, he finished 12 sym-

phonic poems including "Tasso:lamento e trionfo," conceived as an overture to Goethe's *Torquato Tasso* and inspired by Byron's poem; "The Preludes," based on the verses of the poet, Autran, and later referred to a meditation of Lamartine; "Mazeppa," derived from Hugo; "Héroïde funèbre," a funeral march, composed during the Revolts of 1848–1849; "Hungary," an homage to his country; and, "Hamlet" from Shakespeare.

OTHER COMPOSITIONS FOR ORCHESTRA

Excellent scene music masterpieces include *Midsummer Night's Dream,* op. 61 written by Mendelssohn in 1843 as an appendix to the *Overture,* and two works by Schumann, *Szenen aus Goethes Faust* (Scenes of Goethe's Faust), 1843–1853, and the music for *Manfred* by Byron (1848–1851). Berlioz' *The Damnation of Faust,* op. 24 of 1846 is a work halfway between symphony and scene music, meant for the theater. Berlioz has also left works of chamber music that require a huge number of performers, such as the *Grande Messe des Morts,* op. 5 (*Requiem*) (1837) and the *Te Deum,* op. 22 (*Thee, O Lord* [*we praise*]) (1849). Mendelssohn's *Saint Paul* (1836) and *Elijah* (1846), and Liszt's *Die Legende von der heiligen Elisabeth* (*The Legend of Saint Elizabeth*) (1862) are important sacred oratorios. Mendelssohn's ballade, *Die erste Walpurgisnacht,* op. 60 to a text by Goethe, and the lovely poetic works by Schumann, *Das Paradies und die Peri,* op. 50, (*Paradise and the Peri*) of 1843, and *Requiem for Mignon,* op. 98b to a text by Goethe (1849) are remarkable secular works.

THE OPERA

In the German opera, the novelties introduced by Weber in *The Freeshooter* are expanded in *Euryanthe* (Vienna, 1823). The latter perfects the use of recurrent themes to depict characters and situations and leads to a model of the opera without closed numbers (arias, recitatives, duets, and so on) that would be typical of Wagner and of *Oberon* (London, 1826) with refined orchestral colors. Of the other four great romantics, Schumann is the only one to try opera at a late age with *Genoveva,* performed in 1850 when, on the German scene, Wagner's star was already shining.

Meyerbeer made a fortune with his operas *Robert le Diable, The Huguenots,* 1836, and *The Prophet,* 1849. Berlioz added to the genre with *Benvenuto Cellini* (1838) and *The Trojans,* staged in 1863.

The Italians, although energetic, are culturally and stylistically far from the emotions of the romantic movement. Three of them would end their activities in Paris. Rossini left the scene in 1829 with *William Tell,* Bellini died very young in 1835, a few months after the triumph of *The Puritans,* and Donizetti staged his last opera in 1843. Verdi wrote the opera, *The Sicilian Vespers,* with a libretto by Scribe, for the Opéra in 1855. He had already written nineteen operas, among them *Rigoletto, The Troubadour,* and *La Traviata.*

INDEX